Witchcraft in Post-Colonial Africa
Beliefs, Techniques and Containment Strategies

Khaukanani Mavhungu

Langaa Research & Publishing CIG
Mankon, Bamenda

Publisher
Langaa RPCIG
Langaa Research & Publishing Common Initiative Group
P.O. Box 902 Mankon
Bamenda
North West Region
Cameroon
Langaagrp@gmail.com
www.langaa-rpcig.net

Distributed in and outside N. America by African Books Collective
orders@africanbookscollective.com
www.africanbookcollective.com

ISBN: 9956-728-37-3

© Khaukanani Mavhungu 2012

DISCLAIMER
All views expressed in this publication are those of the author and do not necessarily reflect the views of Langaa RPCIG.

Dedication

A Tshivenda idiom warns that when one prospers in life, one should not trample on those that supported one: *Nyavhumbwa wa dagaila, wa kanda vho u vhumbaho*. This book is dedicated to the late Professor Nkhumeleni Victor Ralushai, a tireless mentor to whom I will forever be indebted. Professor Ralushai often pricked my conscience by reminding me that I was more of a sell-out by not writing about our (African) culture than those authors often criticised for having misrepresented it. Sadly he passed away in October 2011, before the publishing of this work. May this book symbolise his intellectual achievement even in death, a testimony of life sacrificed in pursuit of a scholarship devoted to the development of his people.

Table of Contents

Acknowledgements

There is an African proverb which reads: A bundle cannot be fastened with one hand. That is, no one is completely self-sufficient. One constantly needs the support of another for one to succeed in life. My people compel me to acknowledge those that helped me produce this work

I wish to thank Professors John Sharp, Simon Bekker and Francis Nyamnjoh for their guidance and support during this study. I also thank my two research assistants in Cameroon: Bondo Yong and the late Columbus Iyaba. They always believed in this work and showed great enthusiasm. Every village, even the too distant one, was to them always "just over that hill". They knew how to stretch an exhausted mind and take it to greater heights. It was because of them that I was able to walk tens of kilometres to cover many villages in Kom.

I owe much to my wife, Nangula, for her unfaltering love and support, and for always having faith in me. My sources of strength are my lovely daughters, Makhadzi and Masindi, for always believing I am a superman who is capable of scaling down every wall. I thank my mother, a single parent, for her inspiration and for toiling so hard to see me succeed in life.

I am indebted to all the people covered in cases from both Kom and Venda presented in this work. I thank them for retelling their witchcraft experiences, even when they were encountered under very unpleasant circumstances. I thank all the traditional authorities and healers in both Kom and Venda for showing trust in me. To all of them I say "may this work help in making home a peaceful place, particularly when it comes to matters of witchcraft".

Foreword

The core of Mavhungu's book is a spirited rejoinder to the argument that witchcraft killings in post-apartheid South Africa are the result of the global neo-liberal order and its local discontents. Mavhungu rejects the view that these killings have been perpetrated by young people rendered desperate by unemployment and impoverishment turning on elders who are portrayed as having a stranglehold over scarce income. He makes a powerful case for seeing witchcraft killings as one result of the state's failure – both in and beyond the apartheid era – to deal with the experiential reality of witchcraft and with the widespread fear resulting from this reality adequately. By dismissing witchcraft as superstition, existing South African law, which dates back to 1957, leaves people with no measured means to deal with the perceived existence of the phenomenon and the fear it generates, and with little option but to turn to violence to rid themselves of witches.

Mavhungu's thought-provoking analysis is built on an excellent and critical understanding of the literature on witch beliefs in Africa, and on meticulous field research in Venda district in Limpopo Province, South Africa and the chiefdom of Kom in Bamenda district, Cameroon. He makes exemplary use of his comparative material to demonstrate the diversity of beliefs in the power of witches in Africa, as well as the contrasting ways in which people in different parts of the continent deal with the experiential reality of witchcraft.

He shows that people in Bamenda have not made the same recourse to violence in dealing with witchcraft as their counterparts in Venda, largely because local institutions seeking to allay fear and control the activities of witches are still intact.

Yet Mavhungu refrains from suggesting that South Africa should follow Cameroon in giving formal recognition to the reality of witchcraft in a ways that would allow witches to be tried in court for their actions. He argues that Cameroon's attempts to criminalise witchcraft have often been as disruptive of the working of local institutions dealing with witches as the colonial efforts to suppress the phenomenon. The state, he concludes, should not take a position on the reality of witchcraft beyond the recognition that it is an experiential reality to a section of its citizens.

This is an excellent book which analyses complex issues with great insight and economy of expression. It will be of considerable use to scholars, students and the general public.

John Sharp
Professor of Social Anthropology
University of Pretoria
South Africa

Preface

The genesis of this book can be traced back to the tragic incident of 02 October 1990, which divided my village and eventually robbed it of some of its young men and women. While at school on that day, we learnt of the sad news that one of our female colleagues had passed away. Her lifeless body was found hanging from the roof of her parents' house. She left behind no sign, not even a written note, which could provide an explanation for her sudden death.

The days that followed were characterised by organised meetings in the evenings in which some youths tried to make sense of the untimely departure of one of them. Rumour began to spread that witchcraft was to blame for her death: an old woman – a fellow villager and the grandmother of my friend and schoolmate – had cast a spell on the deceased which caused her to hang herself, so it was said. On the evening of Saturday, 06 October 1990, a group of youths snatched the accused old woman from a night vigil, took her outside the yard and stabbed her several times. They then dragged her body to a nearby river where it was doused with petrol before it was set alight.

What followed was the swift arrest of many young men and women from my village. Some were released while others stood trial, accused of plotting and carrying out the murder. The case was heard in a court in Thohoyandou, roughly 40 kilometres away from my village. It was of great interest to me as the accused were youths, most of whom I had played and went to school with. I therefore attended the case from beginning to end. When the case was concluded, I lost seven fellow villagers, friends and colleagues – all between the age of 19 and 33 – to prison.

In addition to the murder case, I also attended, on a Wednesday, a case involving an old man of around 60 years who was accused of threatening to strike with lightning a fellow villager. By so doing, the old man had contravened the Witchcraft Suppression Act of 1957 which made it an offence for a person to pretend to exercise supernatural powers or to impute the cause of certain occurrences to another person. During the proceedings, it was made clear to the old man that his crime was his claim to have access to supernatural powers which he threatened to use to harm a fellow villager. To the surprise of everyone in the courtroom, the old man admitted to the crime and argued that his was not an empty threat but rather a serious warning, which if not heeded, he intended to put to practice. The old man requested anyone in the courtroom to volunteer to be used as an object of a lightning strike. He was shown a tree to strike instead. The old man rejected this stating that his skills and medicines were not to be wasted on the non-livings. He insisted that a human being should be availed for this mission and promised that the procedure would not take more than an hour. However, the demonstration could not be done as no volunteer came forth. The old man was fined R500.

The above cases helped revive lingering questions I had relating to tragic events in my village, often attributed to this occult force: How was it possible that witchcraft could be so prevalent and violent in my society? Why was it that so many people; old and young, literate and illiterate, rural and urban, police and court officials, Christian and otherwise believe in such 'superstition'? What drove educated young men and women to kill in the name of witchcraft? Is the belief in witchcraft held in other societies, and are the consequences similar? Why do some people claim to have access to the use of witchcraft? Is it even possible that one could possess such power? Why is it that, on that Wednesday, no one in the courtroom volunteered to be an object of the experiment on a possible human-made lightning strike?

The above questions about this occult force were the ghosts that haunted me throughout the years. These were the ghosts that had not been laid to rest in 1996 when the Ralushai Commission published its report on the inquiry into witchcraft violence and ritual murders in the Northern Province (now Limpopo) of South Africa. The violence and murders were committed largely in the areas of Gazankulu, Lebowa and Venda in the 1980s. Amongst the recommendations of the Ralushai Report was that: "it would be in the interest of the people and the country (South Africa) to have the abovementioned phenomenon (witchcraft) researched on a more permanent basis… alternatively our universities… should embark on intensive research programmes dealing with witchcraft and ritual killing" (Ralushai *et al.*, 1996:61-2).

The immediate appointment of the Ralushai Commission by the new democratic government was a clear signal that the eradication of witchcraft-related violence was a policy priority of the new decision-makers and policy practitioners in South Africa. This preoccupation with the occult in the policy realm has not diminished. Witchcraft continues to be a social problem for the South African Government. Witchcraft-related cases, some involving violence and loss of lives, are frequently reported across the country. South Africa is actually not alone in this. Witch hunts have become endemic in sub-Saharan Africa. Suspected witches are blamed for "misfortunes, diseases, accidents, natural disasters and deaths. Attacks on witches are commonplace and are viewed as a way to deal with what certain community members perceive as a threat to their community's safety and well-being" (South African Pagan Rights Alliance: 2010).

Similar to observations made in other parts of Africa, witchcraft violence in South Africa is not only limited to the rural areas. In March 2012, residents of Evaton, a township outside Johannesburg, embarked on a violent protest against a pastor of the Rivers of Living Waters Church. The pastor was accused of practising witchcraft which he used to kill people and turn children into snakes. Residents threatened to burn down the church but were prevented from doing so by police.

Notwithstanding the above, the search for a better understanding of witchcraft beliefs and associated violence as well as appropriate policy responses continues. This book, then, arises from an identified need to explore the social context in which witchcraft and associated violence can be understood and contained. It encompasses a comparative study of witchcraft in the kingdom of Venda, South Africa and the kingdom of Kom, Cameroon. The choice for the comparison is based on the hierarchical nature of the traditional political systems in these areas and the differences in the way the state plays a role in the containment of witchcraft-related violence.

This comparative study of witchcraft thus contributes to the on-going debates and attempts to contextualise witchcraft in Africa. It contributes to an understanding of how societies in two different regions of the African continent deal with or contain this occult force and the various possibilities that are open to them. It is also a contribution to the policy discourse in South Africa and the rest of sub-Saharan Africa on the need for governments to develop new policies on witchcraft. Calls are constantly made that the postcolonial state has a moral duty to address the problems that have been created by its predecessor, the colonial state. Unlike its apartheid predecessor, the democratic government of South Africa is expected to formulate a sympathetic policy on witchcraft that is aligned with the Bill of Rights which protects, amongst others, the freedom of belief, religion, conscience, thought and opinion, as well as the freedom to participate in cultural life.

Chapter One

Witchcraft Discourse in Post-Colonial Africa

Introduction

"No person with a background in Western science can admit the reality of witchcraft or the 'breath of men' as defined by the Nyakusa... The only solution is to kill the belief in witchcraft. As we have shown it is somewhat weakened by elementary education and Christian teaching, and we believe that its disappearance turns on increased technical control, particularly in the field of disease, on scientific education, and on the development of interpersonal relations." Wilson (1967:135)

It continues to confound social scientists, policy practitioners and decision-makers that humanity has progressed into the twenty first century without the belief in witchcraft diminishing. In Africa, the "belief in witchcraft is as prevalent as ever. Witchcraft forms part of the basic cultural, traditional and customary principle of Africans..." (Ralushai *et.al.*, 1996:57). Indeed, the belief in witchcraft influences the daily lives of many Africans. It is "ingrained in popular mentality and informs and underscores social, political and cultural beliefs and practices" (Byrne, 2011:1).

Even as Africa is increasingly urbanising and Africans are embracing modern day technological advancement, there is a prevailing common belief across the continent that there are people that have the ability to secretly use supernatural power in order to harm others or to help themselves at the expense of others. These are the witches; they are believed to cause unimaginable horror and destruction, they strike fear and cause a sense of helplessness in communities.

In South Africa, "a large majority of the citizenry believes in witchcraft. The fear of the occult has not faded with apartheid but, surprisingly to many, has only intensified during the transition to

1

democracy. Witch killings rose dramatically in the early 1990s, and since then ethnographic accounts have described an occult epidemic affecting rural and urban areas throughout the country... Attacks on suspected witches continue today, and locals have reported a widespread sense of vulnerability to bewitchment in both city and country" (Tebbe, 2007:186).

It is in this context – when both the majority of the citizenry and a large section of the ruling political elite are believers of witchcraft - that postcolonial Africa has seen the resurgence of calls for state intervention in the occult domain. To those subjected to the wrath of this occult, witchcraft "is perceived to be unjust in much the same way as physical violence. And when citizens are subject to injustice at the hands of others, whether by physical or occult means, they call on government to punish, retaliate and deter. Many Africans feel that such a governmental imperative is particularly strong in a democracy because that form of government carries a special obligation to serve the people and to guarantee them the personal security necessary for the full exercise of political freedoms" (Tebbe, 2007:187).

Immediately after independence in the early 1960s, the Cameroonian State experienced similar calls to address the threat of witchcraft differently. In response, the government enacted the provisions of Section 251 of the Penal Code of 1967 which stipulates that: "Whoever commits any act of witchcraft, magic or divination liable to disturb public order or tranquillity, or to harm another person, property or substance, whether by taking a reward or otherwise, shall be punished with imprisonment from two to ten years, and with a fine of five thousand to one hundred thousand francs."

In 1985, the Cameroonian government went further to commission a study to find out whether witchcraft was a hindrance to development. Thus, "in the case of witchcraft," argues Fisiy (1998:151), "the legislature had sought to contain occult practices by making them a legal offence, a tactic that implicitly acknowledges their existence."

In 2006, Zimbabwe criminalised the practice of witchcraft. The Criminal Law Codification and Reform Act 23 of 2004 prohibits the use of practices "commonly associated with witchcraft." Witchcraft cases may now be dealt with in courts where experts or traditional healers may give evidence as proof that an accused indeed engaged in a witchcraft practice.

In Malawi, there have been calls for government to repeal the Witchcraft Act of 1911 on the basis that it is foreign to Malawians' cultural belief systems as it fails to recognise the existence of witchcraft. Citizen anxiety over witchcraft is widespread, and Malawians have therefore been calling on government to protect them against occult aggression. They are asking for witchcraft to be recognised as real and criminalised (Byrne, 2011:4). In 2009, the Malawi Government established a Special Law Commission to review witchcraft laws of Malawi.

In the democratic South Africa, lawmakers have been under pressure to criminalise the practice of witchcraft (Tebbe, 2007:183). They have, since 1995, been involved in an intensive process of finding solutions to the witchcraft violence that ravaged the countryside, particularly that of the Limpopo (then Northern) Province, in the 1980s. Whereas members of provincial legislatures such as those of Gauteng and Western Cape have been preoccupied with solving crimes such as rape, car hijacking, gangsterism, drug dealing, and housebreaking, those of the Limpopo Province have been more concerned with witchcraft-related crimes.

In an attempt to contain rampant crimes associated with this occult force, the Limpopo Provincial Government appointed an Occult-Related Crimes Unit, which served as a rapid response unit on witchcraft-related crimes. In addition, in March 1995, the Executive Council of the Limpopo Province appointed a Commission of Inquiry into Witchcraft Violence and Ritual Murders in the Northern Province[1]. In its report, the Commission concluded that the Witchcraft Suppression Act No 3 of 1957 "falls short of a pragmatic approach to the issue of witchcraft, and may in fact be fuelling

---

[1]   The late N.V. Ralushai, a professor of Social Anthropology, chaired the Commission and consequently the Commission became popularly known in academic circles as the Ralushai Commission. Its report, which was made public in 1996, will be referred to, in this work, as the Ralushai Report.

witchcraft violence. The government must repeal the Act and introduce legislation that represents a paradigm shift from the current Act, which operates from the premise that denies the belief in witchcraft, leading to the issue being dealt with outside the criminal justice system" (Ralushai *et al.*, 1998:viii). The Commission also recommended the enactment of legislation for the control of traditional healers since their unethical practices contributed to witchcraft violence and ritual murders[2].

The publishing of the Ralushai Report was followed by a number of Government programmes aimed at containing witchcraft across South Africa. In September 1998, the first-ever National Conference on Witchcraft Violence[3], convened by the Commission on Gender Equality, was held in Limpopo Province. The conference recommended, amongst others, the adoption of a National Plan of Action for Eradicating Witchcraft Violence. It also pointed out that the existing Act governing witchcraft had failed to harmonise accuser(s) and accused, and called for legislative reform. In 2004, the Government enacted the Traditional Health Practitioners Act whose purpose was to, amongst others, "provide for the registration, training and practices of traditional health practitioners as wells as to serve and protect the interests of the members of the public who use the services of traditional health practitioners."

To anthropologists, it became an area of focus that the postcolonial South African Government saw it necessary, among its early gestures in office, to appoint a commission of inquiry into witchcraft and ritual murder in the Limpopo Province (Comaroff & Comaroff, 1997:5). Dederen (1996:3) remarked that the Ralushai Report was likely to have a profound effect on debates about future legislation concerning witchcraft in postcolonial South Africa. It

---

[2]   Traditional healers were cited to be at the centre of witchcraft violence. The Commission's Report states that "most of the offences committed by the accused persons, and which arise from the belief in witchcraft, have to do with the influence of diviners and traditional healers...They play a significant role in the commission of crimes based on belief in witchcraft" (Ralushai *et al.*, 1996:48).

[3]   This conference was held in Thohoyandou, former capital of Venda homeland, on 6-10 September 1998.

"presents an important shift from the colonial notion of a civilising mission – which would promote the elimination of witchcraft beliefs – to a new way of speaking about witchcraft in official circles" (Niehaus, 1998:3).

This work therefore provides a response to the on-going question of "what is to be done about witchcraft in the new South Africa?" It is a comparative study of witchcraft in Kom and Venda societies of Cameroon and South Africa respectively. It discusses local variations of witchcraft through a rich collection of detailed cases of witchcraft beliefs, techniques and strategies of witchcraft containment.

Given the hierarchical structure of both societies, the study has been able to investigate why fairly large-scale witch-hunts take place in Venda, while witchcraft does not lead to such violence in Kom. The difference is explained by factors such as the variations in local ideas on witches, differences in the role of traditional authorities, and of state interventions. The study also shows the different trajectories by which local reactions to witchcraft evolve, by describing witchcraft beliefs, the nature of local institutions that deal with witchcraft matters in the two societies, and the impact that State policies on witchcraft have on these local mechanisms of dealing with witchcraft.

The main argument of the book is that interpretations of witchcraft and its manifestations must be informed by the social context of the African community under study, and not be presented as if Africa was a homogenous unit where the reality of witchcraft is the same everywhere. It is observed that most studies have been rather simplistic and dichotomous in this connection, limiting themselves to 'social strain' and 'modernity' thesis, to the detriment of the social context that explain the phenomenon. The Apartheid state in South Africa, by legislating against witchcraft beliefs and practices, incapacitated the community structures that had traditionally contained witchcraft in Venda, thereby occasioning a proliferation of witchcraft-related violence, especially with the advent of a democratic South Africa. It is argued that the relative absence of related violence in Kom could be explained by more sympathetic state policies.

Methodological approach

In carrying out this research, I chose a qualitative approach. A qualitative technique is used to emphasise the roles of insight, discovery, and interpretation rather than hypothesis testing. The important objective was to understand the meaning of experiences of those living in a witchcraft-ridden society, the experience of the accused and accusers, believers and non-believers and how they relate to one another. Patton (1985:1) reminds us that qualitative research is an attempt to "understand situations in the uniqueness as part of a particular context and the interactions there. It is an attempt to understand the nature of the setting ... what it means for participants to be in that setting, ... what the world looks like in that particular setting, and in the analysis to be able to communicate that faithfully to others who are interested in that setting ... The analysis strives for depth of understanding."

Qualitative research assumes that there are multiple realities - that the world is not objective but that it is a function of personal interaction and perception. In order to understand and interpret the subjective reality of the people I set out to study, I had to immerse myself in their world. I thus conducted fieldwork which enabled me to study people in their everyday contexts, gathering data and observing what they do. I became involved in their social world so that I was able to gain access to the meanings that guide their behaviour. This was important since "human actions are based upon, or infused by, social meanings: that is, by intentions, motives, beliefs, rules and values" (Hammersley & Atkinson, 1995:7).

Fieldwork was done in Kom and Venda from January 1999 to December 2001. Amongst the Kom, Fundong, one of the four subdivisions, was chosen for intensive study. Fundong is the administrative centre of the Kom people. It is here where the Kom people first settled on their way from Idjum during what is commonly known as the Boa Track (*Avi A Ngvim*) – an exodus of the Kom people from Babessi. All the Kom people in other subdivisions and in cities outside the Kom area trace their origin to this place. Periodic excursions were, however, made to two other subdivisions –

Njinikom and Belo – for the purpose of comparison and to obtain a comprehensive view of the whole area. In Fundong, I chose the Fundong Traditional Council for observation, and also made several visits to Ngwainkuma Traditional Council.

Besides being an outsider, I found the fieldwork in Kom relatively do-able as the language was not a barrier. Kom is part of the Anglophone area of Cameroon. The spoken language is Pidgin English, which is localised English largely spoken by all the people; young and old, educated and uneducated; in Cameroon. I could understand the language extensively. Where I could not understand, I had the help of my research assistants.

People in Kom were amicable and eager to discuss the experience of black people in South Africa during apartheid and how this impacted on their tradition. It was during social gatherings that one piece of information was traded for the other: I was often the first to tell about South Africa while in exchange they would tell me about their witchcraft experiences. At traditional councils meetings, the elderly people were impressed that for the first time there was a young black researcher, and a South African, who was so interested in the issues of African tradition. They often made it clear that *"we de support plenty de young people dem for Africa laik una whe una laik for savvy we country-fashion. We go give you all de tory whe you want'am forseka we pikin dem go see ya fine work for here and ya combi dem too for usai whe you come-out"*: we are fully supportive of young Africans like you who are interested in our tradition. We will give you all the information you need so that your success can be witnessed by our children here and by your counterparts where you come from.

During meetings, the Kom people were often surprised to learn that there was another society in the southern part of the continent that also held a belief in witchcraft, a belief that was similar to theirs even though with some variations. They were impressed and also felt challenged that they were learning this from a young person who they never expected could be so knowledgeable and interested in matters of tradition. This often seemed to compel them to share extensively their knowledge and experiences. They had to tell more about witchcraft in their society to prove their age and knowledge. In our

7

discussions it became apparent that the knowledge that one exhibited around witchcraft revealed one's age. Those senior elders, like octogenarians, spoke with authority and certain elaboration.

In the early part of this research, however, I experienced some difficulties with regard to obtaining information from traditional healers. They never seemed to understand what I needed from them. A healer would require an exorbitant fee for information on witchcraft-related illnesses. On a bad day, my assistants and I would walk about 20 kilometres to meet healers, only for them to take us to a mountain or river to show us different medicinal plants and explain their uses. This was frustrating and exhausting at times. I however later found out that the misunderstanding was due to the bronze traditional bracelet that I was wearing. I received this bracelet as a gift from my late grandmother upon graduating my Master degree. In South Africa, this gift symbolized love and blessings, a clear statement that I had made my grandmother proud. In Cameroon, however, the bracelet is worn only by traditional healers. This then explained the misunderstanding I initially had with the Cameroonian traditional healers. Even though I told them I was interested in witchcraft issues, they never believed me and still thought that - given my bracelet - I was a healer initiate who was in Cameroon to learn about healing and traditional medicine. It was only after removing this bracelet that this misconception with subsequent healers fell away. The healers who had the misconceived impression confirmed my findings during our follow-up meetings. They were, however, surprised that the bracelet had a different meaning in Venda.

In Venda, the research done was to a large extent what may be called auto-ethnography, that is studying one's own society. Venda is the land where I was born, and an area where I spent my childhood. Not only did I encounter little, if any, difficulty in familiarising myself to local conditions, but my prior knowledge of the area gave me certain advantages that otherwise would not have been the case for an outsider. The fact that Tshivenda – the language used in the area – is my mother tongue, made communication between my consultants and me a lot easier. My consultants were immediately able to identify with and trust me as one of their own, and this led them to discuss with me some of their privileged information. The general response I got during fieldwork was, *"ri takala nga maanda musi ri tshi vhona munwe wa vhana vhashu a tshi takalela zwa sialala. Ri do linga nga ndila dzothe u muthusa uri a kone a ubvetela, ngauralo u do kona u vha tsumbo kha vharathu na dzikhaladzi":* We are impressed to see one of our children being interested in our tradition. We will do everything to support you so you can succeed and become a good example to your brothers and sisters.

The warm reception I received in Venda may also be attributed to the rapport that I had established with most members of some of the communities in the area, particularly traditional leaders and healers. During 1997-8, I had carried out research on traditional healers in the area as part of the work I was doing as a research-intern at the Parliament of the Republic of South Africa. At the time, parliamentarians were involved in a policy-making process around recognition of traditional healers.

There were, however, communities, like those of Makuya and Khalavha, that I had never visited before. To these people and their chiefs I was a stranger, despite the fact that we spoke the same language. They could not trust me enough to discuss such outlawed and sensitive matters as witchcraft. They feared that they would implicate themselves and be charged under the Witchcraft Suppression Act[4]. The ongoing collaboration which I had with the local police[5] helped me gain the trust of these communities. I had to attend village meetings at the chief's residence with members of the South African Police Service (SAPS) from local police stations. These officials introduced me to the villagers and their chiefs, and allayed any suspicion that I was a police or government informer. They pleaded with community members to support me since the work I was doing was likely to aid them. They also indicated that they were also co-operating with me by giving me all the documents that I

---

[4] Act no. 3 of 1957 (as amended in 1970) still applies to the whole of South Africa, and people who are found contravening this law can be prosecuted.

[5] These were members of the Occult-Related Crimes Unit which was supported by Cultural Offices that have been established at local police stations throughout the Limpopo Province.

needed. It was only then that chiefs in these areas were prepared to invite me to their councils, and villagers came forward to tell their stories.

The timing of my fieldwork was another factor that contributed towards making people responsive to the subject of my research. The fieldwork was conducted during the period when these communities had just been ravaged by witchcraft violence that left more than 1000 people dead and many displaced throughout the province. While the violence had subsided, there were still sporadic incidents reported in certain villages. Such tragic occurrences influenced traditional leaders to allow me access to their villages, and to encourage their people to support me, with the hope that my research would be able to shed light on what went wrong with this occult force.

Being a local ethnographer, however, is not always an advantage. One prime element of the anthropological approach in research, which even the foreign researcher is not immune to, is the unpleasant possibility of getting involved in local values. Into this, warns Nukunya (1969:20), "the local ethnographer will find it much easier to be drawn. His naturally unavoidable sympathies for or disapproval of certain institutions may tend to overshadow his scientific desire for an objective appraisal of each situation. This is a weakness which militates against detachment and objectivity unless conscious efforts are made to overcome it." What I write here, owing to my proper training in research methods, is not ethno science but comprises witchcraft accounts that have been subjected to scientific analysis.

I also conducted interviews as a technique of data collection. These were conducted with traditional healers, chiefs, members of the South African Police Service, and individual members of various villages (young and old) who were randomly selected. The format used was a person-to-person encounter. This technique became a necessity during fieldwork in order to assist with clarification of several issues. Interviewing, as Merriam (1991:72) puts it, "is a conversation with a purpose, it is necessary when we cannot observe behaviour, feelings, or how people interpret the world around them. It is also necessary to interview when we are interested in past events that are impossible to replicate."

10

In addition to interviews, group discussions were also conducted in both Kom and Venda. Several discussions were held to ensure that a wide range of community opinion was included. In Kom they were conducted in Ngwainkuma and Fundong villages. In Fundong group discussions were conducted with members of the traditional council, the *fumbuen*[6], and Fundong youth council, comprising eight to twenty five people. In Ngwainkuma group discussions were conducted with members of the traditonal council.

In Venda group discussions were held in Mandiwana, Khalavha, Tshiavha and Makuya villages. In Mandiwana, discussions were conducted with members of the traditional council and senior elders of the village selected by the chief. Discussions were also held with members of the Mphephu Tribal Authority. In Khalavha group discussions were conducted with attendants of the traditional court, while in Makuya discussions were conducted with members of the Makuya Tribal Authority, which consisted of representatives of about 14 villages, the local police station, and transitional local government. In Tshiavha, discussions were held with members of the Tshiavha Royal family. In both societies, there were also group discussions that were held with six to twelve community members at various social gatherings. During several discussions members of a group were assembled according to the same age and background to ensure that they felt at ease with one another and free to state their views openly. In all localities these discussions involved men and women as well as people of all age groups from 14 years upwards. The range of topics varied from witch identities, witchcraft techniques to witchcraft containment.

Studies in Witchcraft

Research should take into account previous work in the same area. An investigator who ignores prior research and theory "chances pursuing a trivial problem, duplicating a study already done, or repeating others' mistakes" (Merriam, 1991:62). Besides providing a

---

[6] Women's secret society

foundation for the problem to be investigated, the literature review can demonstrate how the present study advances, refines, or revises what is already known; thus fulfilling precisely the goal of research that is to "contribute to the knowledge base of the field" (Merriam & Simpson, 1984:30).

The study of witchcraft has its roots in the nineteenth century. During this period, anthropologists took witchcraft in Africa for "evidence of 'primitive' or 'pre-logical' thinking, for something Europeans themselves had, in times past, endured, but had now outgrown. African witchcraft thus served as an unmistakable marker of the 'primitive other'. Africans were mired in a mystical, pre-logical mentality" (Levy-Bruhl, 1926). This idea, meshed with European social evolutionary thinking, was underpinned by Enlightenment notions of progress, development and modernization. Social evolutionary theory assumed that all societies 'evolve' along a linear path from primitive to modern. As societies evolved, a number of things allegedly happened: scientific understanding grew, instrumental rationality increased, a secular world view triumphed, superstitions like witchcraft vanished, and people made an ever clear distinction between facts and fictions, objective truth and subjective falsehood (Moore and Sanders, 2001:2).

In the early part of the twentieth century, Evans-Pritchard (1929, 1935, 1937) challenged the idea that witchcraft was a marker of muddled, mystical thinking and was meaningless superstition. He demonstrated the rationality of witchcraft and argued that Azande witchcraft was a highly coherent and engaged system of meanings – an African epistemology – that made logical sense once one understood the basic premises upon which it was based. The Azande believed in witchcraft because it explained the inexplicable, offered explanations for misfortunes by answering why and not how misfortunes befall certain people, and addressed questions that are ontological and cosmological in nature that called for answers of quite a different order to the narrow answers 'science' could provide.

After World War II, anthropologists (Gluckman 1956; Turner 1957; Mawick, 1965 amongst others) sought understanding of witchcraft by focusing on the social rather than the metaphysical

12

context. They demonstrated how witchcraft led to fissions and, often, fusions in a range of traditional African societies. Witchcraft accusations were an idiom in which the painful process of fission could be set going. Witchcraft accusations were analysed as social stain-gauge, linked to social control and change. According to this group of authors, the distribution of witchcraft accusation between persons in various relationships reveals tension points in social structure, and these tense relations are the prime determinants of the identity of both the accuser and the accused. Since the 1960s, anthropologists and historians (Steadman 1985; Silverbladt 1987) have further developed this theory, primarily through arguing that witchcraft accusations indicate different types of tension in different social contexts.

The general view was that witchcraft accusations tended to occur in situations where social relations were ill-defined or abrasive. Witchcraft was generally interpreted as being the result of new institutions and modern forms of socio-economic breakdown. The rise of witchcraft was frequently linked to colonial meddling in traditional authority structures, increased travel and commerce. Witches in Africa were associated with new forms of consumption, production and political control (Moore and Sanders; 2001:7). "Wherever modern changes have brought about situations for which there are no indigenous precedents, and problems of tribal rules of thumb can offer no solution, there tensions arises and are often expressed in terms of witchcraft" (Marwick, 1958:112).

Meanwhile, African authors were increasingly concerned about the question concerning the reality of witchcraft. Mbiti (1970:9-10) opened a new debate in literature in that he castigated the colonial assumption that witchcraft is a myth which existed only in the mind of the ignorant, and appropriates it as a marker of African identity. Chavunduka (1982) and Motshekga (1984) advocate a new legal approach in which Africans are judged by African norms, and witchcraft comes under the purview of the law. They envisage an important role for traditional courts. Most recently Ralushai *et al.* (1996:45) recommended that "belief in witchcraft and related practices form part of a basic cultural, traditional and customary principle of Africans in South Africa, and Africa as a whole."

Since the 1980s there has been a revival of anthropological study on African witchcraft. Increasingly, African witchcraft, is studied as a modern and not traditional, wide-ranging and not local, historical and not static phenomenon. African witchcraft now operates as part and parcel of modernity itself. It is not only contiguous with but constitutive of modernity. There is a critique of the old ways of focusing on the role of witchcraft beliefs in the maintenance of social order, studying witchcraft's relation to power, but only within the local context, and mostly inside the village. Under serious review is the general tenor of the 1950s that witchcraft beliefs served to denounce overly ambitious leaders and neutralise changes that threatened to undermine the local order. Witchcraft "is basically ambiguous: it not only offers ways of resisting change and concomitant inequalities, but it can also inspire efforts to gain access to new resources" (Geschiere, 1997:217).

This new anthropological analytic "situates African witchcraft within modernity, global capitalism" and accelerating changes in consumerism (Rutherford, 1999:96). It emphasises the examination of, "the signifying practices involved in witchcraft accusations and beliefs and view them as moral registrars of local responses to the wider modern changes of which they are a part," (ibid:97). To the authors of this analytic, the practice of mystical arts in postcolonial Africa has to "do with global processes; or, more precisely, with specific intersections of the global and the local," (Comaroff and Comaroff, 1997:10). Without engaging themselves in the morality of witchcraft, these authors view witchcraft as still serving its traditional function in society, that of helping the modern African to make sense of that which is incomprehensible in his or her daily setting. Common to all these studies is the emphasis on the uncertainties and the continuing relevance of witchcraft discourses in the face of modern changes. The discourses do not express a traditional refusal of change; rather, they try to address modern development and make sense of them (Geschiere, 1997:223). For example, Comaroff and Comaroff (1997:10) state

14

... the dramatic intensification of appeals to enchantment in postcolonial Africa does not imply an iteration of tradition. Per contra, it is often a mode of producing new forms of consciousness, of expressing discontent with modernity and dealing with its deformities; in short, of retooling culturally familiar technologies as new means for new ends. New magic for new situations. It is characteristic of a surging, implosive economy of means and ends popping up all over the planet nowadays, albeit in a wide variety of local guises.

These approaches have also been used to analyse the rampant witchcraft violence that has ravaged the Limpopo Province since the 1980s.[7] In this area, rampant witchcraft violence is seen as a result of:

... widespread anxiety about the production and reproduction of wealth, an anxiety that translated into bitter generational opposition. ... It should be noted, urban "comrades" demonised the parental generation as passive "sell-outs" to colonial oppression ... Precisely this sense of illegitimate production and reproduction pervades youthful discourses of witchcraft in much of South Africa. Many young blacks blame their incapacity to ensure a future for themselves on an aged elite that controls the means of generating wealth without working (Comaroff and Comaroff 1997:19).

Furthermore, witches are depicted as "modernity's metaphors," that is, they are "modernity's prototypical malcontents." The witch serves, once again, as the scapegoat for the neuroses of African society. The actors involved in witchcraft violence, "personify the conflicts of modernity, the ways in which foreign forces invade the

---

[7]   The Limpopo Province is one of the nine provinces of the postcolonial South Africa. The Limpopo Province borders Botswana, Zimbabwe and Mozambique. In the early 1980s, South Africa witnessed a dramatic escalation of witchcraft-related violence, and this province was the most affected. Approximately 1 000 people were killed as a result of both ritual murders and witchcraft accusations in the period between 1980 and 1995 in the province. About 3 000 witchcraft-related cases have been reported in the province since 1994 (Ralushai *et al.*, 1996; Mavhungu, 1999).

local worlds, turning ordinary people into monsters, and endangering established life-ways ... Witchcraft is a finely calibrated gauge of the impact of global cultural and economic forces on local relations," (Comaroff, 1994:9).

However, the tendency to understand and explain witchcraft in terms of dominant explanations – social strain-gauge and modernity – can have its own limitations. This work emphasises the emic, more subjective understandings of witchcraft as an additional way to understanding witchcraft and the violent events that are often associated with it. Boddy (1989:139) remarked that one cannot explain away mystical beliefs in their entirety by merely documenting their instrumental potential. She added that "the argument about social conflict is uni-dimensional and oversimplifies matters: it underestimates the faculty of mystical entities in people's life-worlds, detracts from the polysemy, richness and subtlety of beliefs and does not do justice to the way in which they may alter people's conception of their experiences."

The subjective understanding of witchcraft has found echo in Niehaus' recent exploration of the structural distribution of witchcraft accusations, and his demonstration of why certain accusations were more plausible than others. He cautioned against "the sociological determinism evident in the a priori assumption that social conflict alone is sufficient to determine, or enable us to predict, whom the accuser(s) and those accused of witchcraft would be" (Niehaus, 2001:128). He argued that "the anthropological perception of witchcraft as an idiom of social relations may well obscure rather than illuminate the role of interpersonal conflict in the actual witchcraft accusations. Villagers clearly distinguish between social tensions in general and the types of tensions that they associated with witchcraft" (ibid: 128).

With the use of several cases, Niehaus demonstrated that tense social relations were not always the prime determinants of the identity of both the accuser(s) and the accused. He focused on the views that social actors had of their own situations, and on how individuals subjectively inferred the existence of witchcraft and the identity of alleged witches. "Witchcraft provided individuals with a

16

discourse to conceptualise and articulate otherwise incomprehensible and inexpressible experiences. Emic understandings are essential as they motivate, guide and justify action. Confessions and revelations through divination and dreams were the most authoritative evidence of witchcraft" (ibid: 114).

In line with Niehaus's findings, this study of witchcraft pays close attention to the details of people's narratives. It recognises the emic status of witchcraft as a reality, and acknowledges the importance of circumstantial evidence and paranormal modes of cognition. The study critically re-examines the relationship between witchcraft and the modernity and social strain-gauge explanations. An argument will be advanced in chapter 4 that strained social relations and modernity theories cannot be viewed as the only, or even the most important explanations for the witchcraft violence that took place in the Limpopo Province. Rather, the knowledge and experience that people have about witchcraft is sufficient to trigger an accusation and violent reaction.

An argument will further be made that participation in this witchcraft violence that ravaged Venda and other areas of the Limpopo Province since the 1980s was not shaped by party-political identification, gender or age, but was influenced by fear – the fear of becoming the next victim of witchcraft, and the fear of being labelled a witch. This fear and the awareness of fear cut across all members of community - political leaders, traditional leaders, traditional healers, church leaders, academics, and members of the police service - who were caught up in witchcraft violence.

Geschiere (1997:216) wrote about the influence of fear in witchcraft violence. He discovered that there was an "increasing anxiety among Africans today about witchcraft becoming rampant. In many parts of Africa, this anxiety triggers panicky reactions and a desperate search for new protections to contain novel and therefore all the more frightening witchcraft threats. This search for new protection can have truly shocking consequences."

This book uses ethnographic data collected from two societies that are found in different countries – one in the southern African region and another in the west African region – of the African continent, to systematically show how, given such fear, people in

17

witchcraft-ridden communities contain witchcraft daily. Recent work on the containment of witchcraft has tended to limit comparison to different regions of the same country. This is true of a study by Geschiere and Nyamnjoh (1998) on the relationship between witchcraft, democratisation and the politics of belonging in Africa, which was confined to comparing data collected from two culturally different regions of Cameroon. With this comparison, the two authors explored the different trajectories by which urban-rural relationships evolve, and provided an understanding of the often desperate efforts people make to contain witchcraft and the various possibilities open to them. They suggested that in some contexts more than others, concrete means seem to be available to try and contain witchcraft. They demonstrated this with a case of the Bum people of the North-West Province who, despite being in diaspora in the faraway South West Province, still appealed to their Foyn (chief) at home when witchcraft seemed to be proliferating amongst them.

Several authors have written on the containment of witchcraft by various states and their people. Fisiy (1998) explored different methods employed during the colonial era to deal with witchcraft. He then showed how the Cameroonian state, especially in the East Province, was using a combination of legal, administrative, and political tools to contain witchcraft. He indicated that since 1980, the state courts had launched a true judicial offensive against witches, and they relied on the testimonies given by traditional healers to establish proof. The author found this position very controversial. Meyer (1998) however, discussed a form of containment that has proved surprisingly successful in many parts of Africa. She demonstrated the role of the Pentecostalists in exorcising witchcraft in Ghana. In her study in coastal Kenya, Ciekawy (1998) showed how the Mijikenda forms of witchcraft control were used by state authorities in the process of state formation. She showed how the combined effort of local people, politicians and administrator to contain witchcraft helped produce new social, cultural, legal and political identities during this process. A year later, Douglas (1999) demonstrated – using the Lele of the Kasai – that some societies have and support "institutions whose express purpose in to detect, disable, and punish

18

sorcerers." She described the anti-witchcraft movement headed by two Catholic priests that occurred in the late 1970s and early 1980s.

Organisation of the book

Chapter 2 compares the belief in witchcraft in both Kom and Venda. This comparison reveals the variation in people's ideas about witches, and serves to explain the differences in witchcraft violence in both societies. Following such a variation in witchcraft belief, an argument is made that the use of expressions like "African witchcraft" to refer to witchcraft belief in various parts of the African continent can be misleading in that this belief is neither homogeneous nor coherent.

Chapter 3 deals with strategies that are used to contain witchcraft in both societies. It shows local measures employed to contain witchcraft at family and community levels, and how these mechanisms are impacted upon by witchcraft policies of both the South African and Cameroonian States.

Chapter 4 focuses on the explanation of witchcraft violence in Venda by testing the existing theoretical approaches against the empirical material generated by this study. The social strain and the modernity theories are found to be insufficient for explaining the dynamics of witchcraft violence in Venda. It is demonstrated that social stress may be a result rather than a cause of witchcraft accusations and violence. The political context, specifically the outlawing of witchcraft accusations is seen as the main reason for the polarization and violence associated with witchcraft in Venda. It is indicated that communities became united against witches, across age, gender and class divisions. The role of fear and the subjective understating in the witchcraft violence is emphasized and backed up with a discussion of cases. It is argued that in a situation where the traditional authorities were incapacitated through the action of the state, the killing of witches in Venda became the alternative form of dealing with the situation.

In concluding, chapter 5 gives an overview of the study and provides recommendations to the South African Government with

19

regard to developing a policy on witchcraft. An argument is made that, amid the increasing calls for the postcolonial South African state to redress the past injustices brought about by its apartheid predecessor in the occult domain, the Witchcraft Suppression Act of 1957, as amended in 1970, should be completely repealed. The Act should however not be substituted by a law that recognises and seeks to control witchcraft, as suggested by witchcraft believers.

Chapter Two

Witches of Venda and Kom

The Omnipresence of Witchcraft

Although the Kom and the Muvenda live in the African continent in localities that are geographically apart, they both exist in worlds that are engulfed with constant fear of witchcraft. During fieldwork in both Kom and Venda, I came to realise that the belief in witchcraft permeates almost every aspect of life; be it social, political, religious, economic or judicial. My first six months of research in Venda demonstrated this omnipresence of witchcraft. On the morning of Saturday, 8 January 2000, I was attending the funeral of a businessman in a village just outside Mphephu's palace.[8] There was already a rumour circulating that he had been bewitched by people who were jealous of his entrepreneurial success. In the afternoon of Sunday, 12 March 2000, I was at the Thohoyandou[9] Stadium attending a MTN League game that involved a local soccer team and another from Gauteng. Here I overheard one of two young males seated behind me whispering to the other 'that witch, that witch', and pointing at a man who was walking towards the stand. Further on my right side, I saw three more people pointing their fingers at the same man. I later learnt that they were pointing at a teacher who narrowly escaped death when students stoned him after accusing him of causing the death of another teacher at Mphephu High School.

The following Sunday in a traditional court under Makuya Tribal Authority, villagers were praised for the calm and peace that prevailed in the village over the past seven months. The reason, it was said, was that during this period there was no single witchcraft incident reported. Thursday, 30 March 2000: I listened to a talk-show, hosted

---

[8] Mphephu was the first President of the Venda homeland. He died in 1986 and was rumoured to have been poisoned by a member of his cabinet.
[9] Thohoyandou was the capital city of the former Venda homeland. It is now one of the towns of the Far-North region of the Limpopo Province.

by the local university radio, on the topic of witchcraft and its legal status, an issue that was the subject of the workshop and National Conference on Witchcraft held in the Province the previous year.

The first week of April 2000 witnessed a cover story on *Mirror* (April 7, 2000), a local weekly newspaper, that read 'a pensioner, Johannes Singo (82), who lived in constant fear following threats by community members who accused him of suspected witchcraft practices, decided to end his own life by hanging himself at his yard in Lwamondo'. Then came the Easter holiday, and the Provincial Traffic department launched Operation *Ndadzi* (lightning) as part of its campaign to reduce road accidents, and in so doing, tapped into and increased the notoriety that witchcraft-related lightning had in the Province.

On Monday, 1 May 2000, I was woken by a call from a member of the Executive Council of a traditional court in a village 10 kilometres outside Thohoyandou who informed me that a 34-year-old man had killed his uncle whom he accused of witchcraft. 'Witches in exile: superstition and fear have kept the residents of Tshitwi isolated for almost a decade', read a headline in the *Sunday Times* of 21 May 2000, one of the largest national newspapers in South Africa. On 13 June 2000, Radio Phalaphala[10] reported in its 11h00 am news bulletin that the Amnesty Committee had granted 38 prisoners amnesty for witchcraft-related crimes. On Sunday, 18 June 2000, I attended a church service during which the pastor delivered one of the congregants from witchcraft.

The examples cited above are an apt reflection of the extent to which witchcraft permeates popular discourse in Venda. Witchcraft exists in newspapers, on television, amongst relatives, in prisons, in schools, at soccer games, in churches, in government, on the roads, at conferences, at funerals, amongst 'us' and even in demarcated areas.

In Kom, the experience was similar. Witchcraft was a constant feature of the discourses in the homesteads, classrooms, social gatherings, market squares, traditional council meetings, community

---

[10] This is the only radio in South Africa that broadcasts in Tshivenda. Most people in the rural areas still depend on the radio as a source of information.

work and death celebrations, just to mention a few. The witchcraft discourse revolved around the terrible deaths of ordinary citizens as a result of their encounters with witches at night, the trapping of a naked witch at dawn in other peoples' homestead, the indefinite desertion or non-use of a farming plot as a result of an alleged witch who had buried medicine in it in order to kill the next person who may use such a plot for any purpose, the ostracism or banishment of an alleged witch, and various tombs in front of impressive modern houses that signify that the owners had been killed by jealous villagers.

In both societies, tragic incidents related to witchcraft practices and accusations were recounted to me on an almost daily basis. I often came across the traumatised victims of witchcraft accusations; some of whom still bear either the psychological or physical scars that serve as a reminder of the existence of the belief in witchcraft. It was after meeting several members of these societies that I began to understand the multifaceted nature of the fear of witchcraft. On the one hand, it is the fear of the attack of witches, while on the other; it is the fear of being branded a witch, which is equally dreaded. It is in this context that every villager is neither above witchcraft suspicion nor immune from becoming a victim of witchcraft attack.

It is incidents such as these that make African witchcraft a constant subject of academic debate and research. But in our daily discourse about African witchcraft, how often do we ask ourselves: "what is African witchcraft really?" Unlike Europe and America, Africa is culturally a very complex continent. It consists of more than fifty countries and several hundred languages and ethnic groups. It is a place where both the lowest and highest standards of living are found; "the forms of political organisation range from informal patterns of leadership in hunting and gathering bands to divine kings and bureaucratic states. African ways of making a living range from hunting and gathering, through complex agricultural systems using irrigation, to highly specialised craft industries. If such variations can be found in the 'objective' circumstances of language, politics, social organisation, and modes of livelihood, how different must be the

23

products of the imagination, the ways that Africans have developed of understanding and thinking about their world" (Karp 1995:211)?

Given this vastness of the African continent, is it possible to have a belief in witchcraft that is homogeneous and coherent? In other words, are witches in various African localities identical? Who are the African witches and where do they derive their powers from? What are their techniques of bewitchment? All these are matters that I delve into in this chapter. I aim to show that although "African witchcraft" is used to refer to the belief in witchcraft that is found in the African continent, there are variations in this belief, and that these variations can be attributed largely to the context – cultural and social – within which it is found in various African localities. I will demonstrate this by a comparison between the data of the Kom and Vhavenda. First, a general introduction of Kom and Venda is considered.

Kom

Kom is a West African Kingdom situated in the central highlands of the Cameroon Grassfields. The Grassfields stretches continuously and lies between 4^0 15' and 7^0 N and 9^0 and 11^0 15' E. The kingdom was founded before the nineteenth century, and has an area of 280 square miles and occupies a high mountain terrain with an average height of 5000' above sea level (Nkwi, 1976:11). Kom is actually an extension of the Bamenda highlands in the Boyo division of the North-West Province. Here the Kom people are settled in three valleys – Bello, Njinikom and Fundong – which are separated from one another by mountains and hills. The kingdom's capital, Laikom, perches on a spur at a height of 6324'. To the north, Kom shares borders with Bum and Bafmeng, to the west with Bafut, and to the south with the Babanki and Ndop chiefdoms. There are Oku and Nsaw chiefdoms in the east.

The word Kom refers to people who live in and originate from Kom. These people speak a language called Itanghikom, which bears a resemblance to Bantu and Sudanic languages (Kaberry, 1952). The people are known to belong to the so-called Tikar group. The power structure in Kom consists of territorial rulers such as the foyn (king), chiefs, village and ward heads. Succession to kingship, chieftainship, and village headship is based on descent. The foyn is the head of all the Kom people and personifies his kingdom. He is the religious head of his people and still enjoys most powers in traditional matters. His palace is said to be sheltering royal shrines for the temporal and spiritual welfare of his people.

Map 1: The ten provinces of Cameroon [including the Kingdom of Kom]

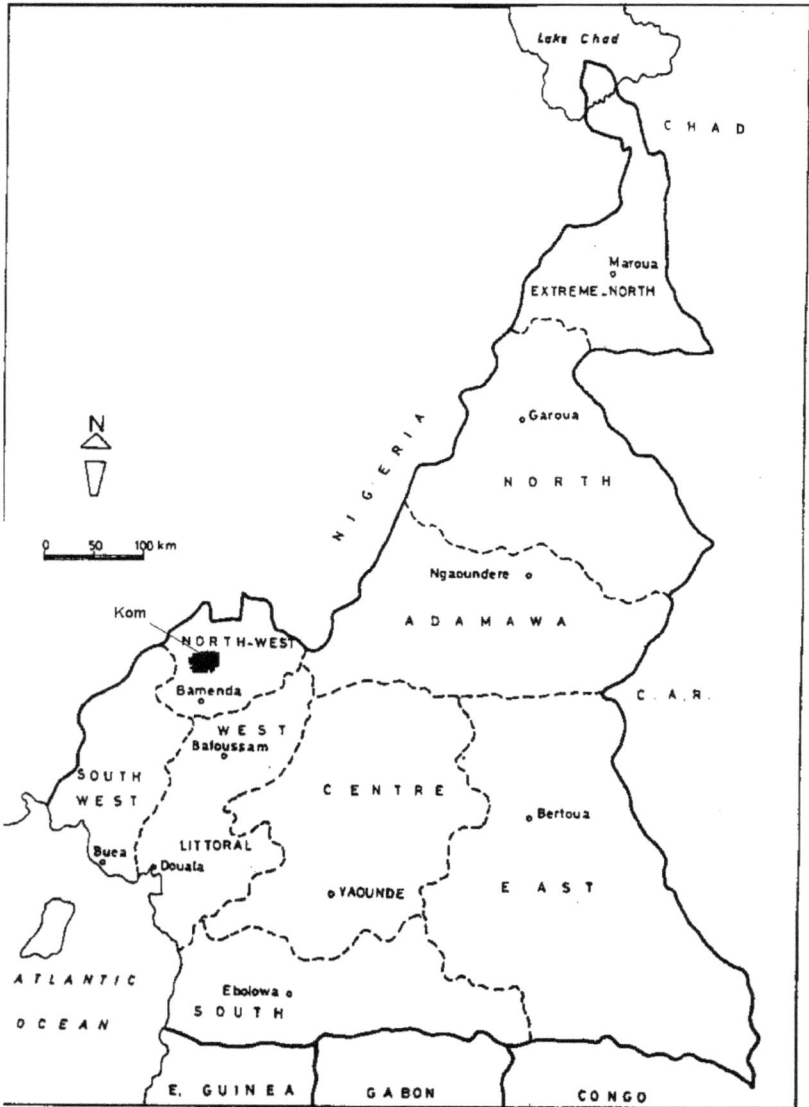

Source: Fanso (1989:176)

Kom has two climatic seasons just like many areas in the high Savannah belt. The dry season is from November to March, while the rainy season runs from April to October. June and August are the wettest months. The type of agriculture practised in Kom is subsistence farming. Besides the fact that people also plant in and around their homesteads, there are peasant holdings that are located around 20 kilometres from the settlement. Here people still practise traditional agriculture, which involves the use of hoes, sticks and cutlasses. A polyculture is practised with nearly all the crops grown on the same plot. Maize is the dominant crop, followed by beans, plantains, bananas, cocoyams, sweet and Irish potatoes, cassava and groundnuts. The Njinikom Co-operative Union at Wombong is the only semblance of an industry. It employs hundreds of people, a number which swells in summer when vacationing students are employed for holiday jobs, and during the season when the Co-operative is processing coffee (Nkwi, 1997).

Venda

Venda is a kingdom in the Far-North region of the Limpopo Province of South Africa. It originated as far back as around the 1720s, during which the Vhavenda were under one king called Thovhela (Beach, 1980). The area lies between $29^0 - 32^0$ E, $22^0 - 24^0$ S. Its surface area is 6 500 km². Venda borders Zimbabwe in the north, Malamulele in the east, and Botlokwa in the west and south. The area comprises a broken mountainous terrain with the Soutpansberg range stretching from east to west. A number of rivers flow through the area. The major rivers are the Nzhelele, Nwanedi and Mutale. The major towns are Makhado and Thohoyandou.

Map 2: The nine provinces of South Africa [including the Kingdom of Venda]

Source: Niehaus (2001: xv)

The name Venda refers to an area occupied by people called Vhavenda, who speak a language called Tshivenda. Homogeneous as they may be, Vhavenda have several clans. These are the Vhangona, Vhambedzi, Vhalembetu, Vhatavhatsindi, Vhatwanamba, Vhalovhedzi, Vhakwevho, Vhaluvhu, Vhalaudzi, Masingo, and

Vhalemba. The Vhavenda have always maintained a clear hierarchy. At the head is a king (*Thovhela*) who rules the whole nation. Then under a king, are chiefs who head villages. These chiefs are largely related to the king. Depending on the size, each village could be divided into sub-villages under the headmen (*vhakoma*). Each sub-village then comprises a number of homesteads (Mabogo, 1990:22).

Venda has a subtropical climate with the annual rainfall ranging from 200 to 300 mm. Mean summer temperatures vary between 24⁰C and 30⁰C, while mean winter temperatures may be between 15⁰C and 24⁰C. The highest rainfall is in summer. The form of agriculture practised is largely subsistence farming. The main crops produced are maize, millet, groundnuts, grain sorghum, sweet potatoes, beans and peas. The main industrial crop is tea at the Thathe Vondo Tea Plantation (Malan & Hattingh, 1976:233). The plantation offers employment opportunity to most Vhavenda, even though on a temporary basis.

Witchcraft beliefs and practices

Belief in witchcraft contends that evil forces in society can be manipulated by specially endowed individuals to the detriment of ordinary people. It holds that every community since the beginning of time has contained people with malevolent intentions, who cause havoc during their lives and whose spirits after death select suitable individuals – witches – to possess and endow with wickedness (Holland, 2001:7).

Unlike Western religions, African thought does not conceive the source of evil to be a fallen god or spirit like Satan or the Devil. Instead, the source of evil is located in the human world among the ambitious and jealousies of men [and women]. The source of evil is thus demonic humanity: the witch or sorcerer (Benjamin Ray cited in Holland, 2001:186).

In both Kom and Venda, witchcraft is an evil act performed by people through the use of medicines of plant or animal origin in order to harm others and their belongings. Witches inflict this harm by manipulating natural events through the use of supernatural

29

means. In their act of bewitching, witches employ various techniques with deadly consequences in all aspects of life. This explains why witchcraft is held accountable for almost all inexplicable misfortunes.

Most African societies, as Mbiti (1969:197) tells us, "do not often draw the rather academic distinction between witchcraft, sorcery, evil magic, evil eye and other ways of employing mystical power to do harm to someone or his or her belongings." This is the case in Kom and Venda. Amongst the Vhavenda *vhuloi* is an all-inclusive word for supernatural acts. Similarly, one finds *evung* being the all-embracing concept amongst the Kom.

In Kom and Venda, witchcraft is omnipresent, a threatening force during day and night. During the day, witches bury medicines in the ground and even put poison in their victim's food. Their intention is to kill or bring eternal suffering to the victim. At night, witches go into trance or transform into an animal through which they bewitch while their bodies lie passively in their sleep. Witches love the night: they are most active at night while ordinary souls are deep in their sleep. They eat, throttle, beat and even enslave their victims in their sleep. An early morning fatigue is often blamed on witches. It is believed that witches usually work one hard at night; that is, they take one with them to their fields for planting or harvesting.

Unlike in Zandeland (Evans-Pritchard, 1937) where it is believed that witchcraft can only be inherited, in both Kom and Venda there is a belief that witchcraft can also be acquired through a purchase. These differences are evident in the morphology of witchcraft in the three societies. In Zandeland one can pin-point the spot in the witch's body where witchcraft is located. In Venda, one's heart determines one's potential to become a witch. *Muthu ha ngo tea u vha na mbilu mmbi*: a person is not supposed to have an evil heart, so goes the Tshivenda saying. It is believed that if one has an evil heart that always wishes other people ill, one risks buying witchcraft in order to harm others. Similarly, an evil heart is the trigger that activates an inherited witchcraft that lies dormant within one. In Kom, moral vices such as ill-heartedness, jealousy and greed are the ones that determine one's involvement in witchcraft. Excessive desire by others

30

to have too much agricultural land drives them into using witchcraft to kill their siblings. The notion of *djambe* – a force or being that is found in the belly of a person and permits its proprietor to automatically transform into a spirit or animal that would do all sorts of things supernaturally – as we know it from the Maka of eastern Cameroon (see Geschiere, 1997) is not common amongst the Kom.

In both societies, any person designated to become a witch will still have to be carefully nurtured in the skills of witchcraft. Within a family with a history of witchcraft, a relative may teach another the techniques of bewitchment. Common cases involve parents teaching their children. For instance, a parent would choose to teach a child that he or she loves or favours the most. There is also a gender aspect to this teaching: male and female witches are said to teach sons and daughters respectively.

In Kom, parents initiate their children into witchcraft by carrying them on their back in an upside-down position when they are going out to *chop* (eat) others with their witchcraft. Such children usually confess to friends that on arriving at the victims' homesteads, their parents tied them upside-down to a tree. They claim that they heard people screaming in their beds while being beaten by their witch parents. In Venda, children that are undergoing witchcraft lessons are associated with hallucination. The children often tell their peers that they used them as riding horses at night, or that there was a galley at night and they used other children as a bridge to cross. In both societies, these children are given certain medicines to stop them from revealing nightly adventures.

In Kom and Venda a distinction is not drawn between a male and female witch. The word witch is used inclusively. The Vhavenda generally use the word *muloi* (pl. *vhaloi*) to refer to either a male or female witch, while the equivalent word used by the Kom is *avung* (pl. *evung*). If one asks for gender differentiation of an *avung*, the Kom will add *avung a lumna* (male witch) or *avung a kia* (female witch). The Vhavenda will similarly state *muloi wa munna* (male witch) or *muloi wa musadzi* (female witch). The witch and the wizard, as we know them from the literature, cease to exist.

31

There is however, a certain witch called *tshivhimbili* amongst the Vhavenda. This is a male witch (and not a wizard) with certain unique characteristics that distinguish him from other male witches. Apart from being notoriously known for visiting his female victims at night to have sex with them while they are in deep sleep, *tshivhimbili* is also known for his leadership qualities: he leads witches (both males and females) in their ceremonies or when they harm their victims. The Kom equivalent of *tshivhimbili* is *foyn evung* (king of witches). The witch is so powerful that he overcomes most of the medicines that would otherwise trap witches. He is credited with extensive knowledge of traditional herbs, particularly those used for evil purposes. Like *tshivhimbili*, *foyn evung* can transform into various witchcraft familiars. His role in sexual matters is however not as established as that of *tshivhimbili*. *Foyn evung* can only be detected in the act of bewitching by *ngambe* (traditional healers) in their shrines. *Ngambe* see the *foyn evung* when they pour palm wine in their sacred gourds. Both *tshivhimbili* and *foyn evung* cannot be cleansed of their witchcraft.

In Kom and Venda, it is believed that a witch is aware of his or her supernatural powers and can cause harm by cursing someone. This belief is reflected in some of the statements that the Vhavenda and Kom are encouraged to refrain from making. These are the statements that are often attributed to people who are boastful of their witchcraft. For instance, one is not allowed to make statements such as "you shall see": *ni do zwivhona* in Tshivenda; and *wa nyanah* in ItanghiKom. In both localities, these statements are interpreted as "an ominous sign of an impending witchcraft attack"; expressions that, even when unaccompanied by any physical action, "constitute verbal missiles that could kill" (Fisiy 1998). When such a statement is made during a quarrel it is implied that the matter is not resolved and that the source of the statement will resort to witchcraft. The Ralushai Report cites cases of people who used to declare their

32

witchcraft in public, and were later caught in other people's homesteads[11].

Holland (2001:9) observed that in some African countries a person "may verbally abuse another person in a fit of jealousy, by saying something like 'I wish you were dead!' If harm thereafter befalls the other person angrily cursed in this way, suspicion of witchcraft may fall on the one who did nothing more than express hatred. So anybody is haplessly capable of committing witchcraft..."

Menacing as this occult force may be considered in both societies, it is however believed that the "designation" to become a witch is not inescapable. A good heart can save the supposed inheritor or trainee from practising witchcraft. It can prevent a child from going along with its parents to the supernatural world to learn witchcraft. Even if a child is designated to become a witch – by making incisions and applying medicines around its waist so that it automatically becomes a witch when it grows – being good-hearted will give the child the capability to defy the witchcraft forces. There are cases where good-hearted inheritors or trainees of witchcraft do at a later stage consult traditional healers for cleansing.

Inherited witchcraft

In both Kom and Venda, inherited witchcraft involves deities who are known for their rapacious demand for human soul. The spirits are either inherited or passed over to a victim in the form of a spell through ritual incantation. Once inherited, the spirits operate in conjunction with their human master In this case, the master hands over human beings, most of whom die from strangulation, as an offering to the spirits. In reciprocity, the spirits enable their master to trade souls with witch familiars such as hyenas, polecats, snakes, and *tokoloshi*. Thus, a witch's soul leaves his or her body, usually at night, and goes into that of a witch familiar so that the witch will be able to perform his or her evil act at a

---

[11]The Ralushai Commission documented a case of Jim Nephalama, a reputed wizard in Fefe village, Venda, Limpopo Province, who used to boast that he could do whatever he liked with other people.

desired pace and without being recognised or getting caught. Incidents of witches being caught naked in other people's homesteads, usually at dawn, are not unusual in villages around Venda. However, if one kills a witch familiar in the act of bewitching, the passive body of the concerned witch back home also dies instantly.

This type of witchcraft is not only limited to the Vhavenda. In a study of the Green Valley in Limpopo Province, Niehaus (2001:51) noted the existence of witches with familiars in the area. The popular familiar in the area was the *tokolotsi*. Informants "portrayed an essential unity between the witch and the *tokolotsi*. They maintained that when the familiar is killed the witch would also die. This is because the witch assumes the form of the familiar, uses the same fat as it does and because there is a mystical inter-dependence of their identities."

Case 1: Makwarela: A witch with spirit-induced witchcraft in Venda

Nndwammbi[12] was a well-known professional hunter who lived in Muomvani village. In the same village lived Makwarela, a notorious witch who could change herself into a hyena. One day Nndwammbi left with his dogs for hunting at around 02h00 in the morning. On his return from hunting at around 05h00, Nndwammbi spotted a hyena near the homesteads, and his dogs started a chase. After a struggle the hyena succumbed to the dogs. Meanwhile, in one homestead people were woken up by Makwarela, who was screaming *ni nndumiselani nga mmbwa dzanu*: why do you let your dogs bite me? Villagers who gathered around to help Makwarela were shocked because they could not see any dog despite the fact that Makwarela

---

[12] Some of the names of places and people I cite in this book have all been changed to preserve the anonymity of the individuals whose personal lives and tragic fate I evoke or discuss here. Despite the recommendation of the Ralushai Commission and the resolutions of the National Conference on Witchcraft, that the Witchcraft Suppression Act should be repealed, the Act is still in existence in South Africa. This has led to the real names of some villages and traditional councils being withheld, so as to protect the identity of those parties involved.

was screaming uncontrollably in pain and eventually died. When Nndwammbi was walking past Makwarela's homestead he was greeted with the news of her death. When he told the people that his dogs had just killed a hyena, those present dispersed whispering that the witch has finally run out of luck[13].

The above case exemplifies how the life of a witch who has inherited witchcraft can be abruptly ended by the killing of a witchcraft familiar. According to the Ralushai Report, Jim Nephalama, a self-confessed witch in Fefe Village in Venda, was killed in the form of a strange animal that later changed into a full human being. The killing took place when Naledzani Netshiavha and his wife were, on the night of 20 September 1985, woken up by a scratching sound on the door of their hut. After the couple's repeated inquiries as to who was causing the sound were met with no response, Naledzani picked up an axe and opened the door. As he was about to walk out of his hut Naledzani saw a strange animal that looked like a bat hanging from the rafters of the roof of his hut. He chopped it and the animal fell to the ground. The couple went to call their two relatives. On their return, they found the chopped animal crawling towards the fence of Naledzani's yard. Naledzani then chopped the animal until he was sure it was dead. The four then called other villagers to come and help identify what kind of animal it was. Several people including the village chief arrived at the scene and described the animal differently. The descriptions vary from a bat, donkey, to just another 'thing'. Gideon Netshiavha, Naledzani's brother who was a taxi driver, arrived and then directed the lights of his taxi at the dead animal. By this time, a number of villagers had

---

[13] Makwarela's granddaughter, Tsumbedzo, lost her marriage due to witchcraft. She had two miscarriages since her return from her in-laws. Two days before her last miscarriage, Tsumbedzo gave a 20 cent coin to Mulalo's son. At night the son started hallucinating and staring at the rooftop, screaming that he was seeing a huge animal. Mulalo immediately suspected that the coin passed over to her son was a vector of witchcraft, and that her son was marked as a victim for the spirits so that Tsumbedzo could deliver. Mulalo immediately confronted Tsumbedzo and warned her that she was aware of the gift of 20 cents and that Tsumbedzo would be responsible for anything that happens to her son. A moment later, Mulalo found that her son was better. Two days later, Tsumbedzo miscarried.

already arrived. To the surprise of everyone at the scene, the dead animal transformed into the body of a child with an adult head. Suddenly the body morphed into that of an adult, and villagers were shocked to discover that the dead person was Jim Nephalama, an old man in his seventies. There were three fatal blows to his head (Ralushai *et al.*, 1996:191-2).

In Kom, it is however believed that even if the familiar is killed, the witch may still survive what in Venda would amount to an inescapable death. The survival is dependent on the witch's success to retrieve the dead familiar. Once the familiar is killed, the witch becomes immediately immobilised. While in this state, the witch directs a relative to a particular homestead to retrieve the dead animal. If the dead familiar is returned to the witch, then he or she escapes what would be imminent death. It is for this reason that the Kom would usually burn all animals associated with witchcraft upon killing them. The Kom people are however not elaborate on what the witch does once the dead animal is returned to him or her. It is said that the dead familiar is left with the witch in solitude, and that the next time the witch appears in public, he or she is in a healthy state. The case below was recounted to me to demonstrate the existence of inherited witchcraft in Kom. It took place in Fanantui, a village under the Njinikom subdivision, around 8 kilometres from Laikom.

Case 2, Bea: A witch with spirit-induced witchcraft in Kom

For a week Ngàm had been woken up by a mewing cat. Each time he opened the door, the cat mewed and entered the house. Ngàm suspected there might have been rats in his house which the cat was after. The following day, Ngàm, his wife and children thoroughly cleaned the house. The mewing cat, however, continued to visit the homestead for about a week. Ngàm consulted a healer who told him that the cat was a witchcraft familiar that should be killed. The cat was supposed to bewitch Ngàm and his family, but was mewing as a result of the medicinal protection that a healer administered around Ngàm's homestead. The healer gave Ngàm some medicines to smear on his body before he killed the cat. One

36

morning Ngàm killed the cat. Meanwhile Bea – a notorious *foyn evung* – started perspiring and requested his daughter to retrieve the dead cat that was in Ngàm's house. On arrival at Ngàm's homestead, Bea's daughter found Ngàm burning the dead animal. She attempted to flee but was caught and eventually confessed that her father had sent her to retrieve the dead cat. Ngàm took the girl back to Bea's house. On arrival, they found that the old man was dead. Ngàm then reported the case to the *bonte's* (chief's) compound.

Purchased witchcraft

There is also a belief that witchcraft can be purchased by those that do not have a history of the occult force in their families. *Hovho ndi vhuloi ha u renga*: that is the witchcraft acquired through buying, as it is often said in Venda. This explains why everyone can become a suspect of witchcraft. Evil-hearted people pay a fee for lessons, herbs and methods of bewitching received from a witch master. Purchased witchcraft may however get out of control with deadly consequences for the purchaser. It may constantly demand from the purchaser a human sacrifice, especially children, siblings or any other relative. Incidents of family members dying in succession because a relative who bought witchcraft has sold them out are not uncommon in Kom and Venda.

In Venda, witches in this category hold meetings at identified places. They spend the night having strange dances outside the houses of those they hate. They dance until they are dizzy and fall down like people in a trance. They form clubs and societies with strong leadership, while collaborating in their nightly errands. Members in these groups are usually experts in different departments of bewitching. Misbehaving or withdrawing membership is unacceptable. When displeased by their own member, these witches may decide to turn him or her into a sacrifice. Once they decide to take the life of one of their own, they congregate at night; move to and from the member's homestead while singing *hogo*, a popular song for male circumcision. When ordinary people hear the singing of *hogo* around midnight, they know the death of a witch is imminent.

37

These witches have their own army that they deploy at night to fight witch armies from other villages. *Vhaloi vha a bva pfumo* (witches discharge the spear), so goes the Tshivenda saying. They challenge each other and fight as a means of testing their powers. Sometimes the battle is territorial: witches of different groups are believed to reach rapport over territories of bewitchment and that a battle is waged once a breach occurs. The battle is fatal: the injured witch cannot be cured; the result is death. Villagers recognise the fighting field by the drops of blood and footprints that are scattered on it in the morning. If one sees witches in their nightly errands, during a fight or wrestles a witchcraft familiar, one gets numbed into an indifferent moron. When people wake up in the morning to find one showing signs of numbness and indifference, they hurriedly take one to a healer for immediate de-anaesthetisation.

In Kom, either a friend or relative initiates one into a witch society. Once being a member of the witch society, a witch initiate may be asked to pledge a relative or a loved-one as a sacrifice. The society is called the *Muso* – a supernatural world where members get things to bring back to their homes. This society is located at the Ijim Mountains just above Laikom. Witches go to the *Muso* in trance, where on arrival they are given *meyi* (a yellow soup). Once they drink the *meyi*, they automatically become initiated into the *Muso*.

Annually a witch may bring back from the *Muso* riches like money, good harvest and fertility to their families. Conversely, they may bring back misfortunes like disease, famine or deaths. This is dependent on the content of the bundle that a witch chooses randomly after eating and dancing. Thus, a witch who chooses a bad bundle may bring back home a bad harvest, resulting in poor yields, plague or other dangerous things to his or her family.

During fieldwork, the crop yield in Kom was high with people filling two barns. This was attributed to two women friends in the Kom area. One of the women had invited the other to a *Muso* society. The friend agreed but on the night of departure she was taken away by an uncle who arrived unexpectedly from the city. The friend who was already a *Muso* member then left alone for the *Muso*. On her return with the bundle she went to her friend to show her the corn seeds that she had found. The friend asked to be given some since it was not her fault that the friend could not wait for her. The lucky friend refused and this was followed by a chase. As the two women were running after each other the seeds were dropped over Kom (beyond the lucky woman's farming plot). This then became the yield for everyone in the Kom area.

A member of the *Muso* can be saved if bathed with medicinal herbs. A traditional healer places a chicken on the member's head to determine the success of cleansing. If the chicken remains, then nothing can be done to save the witch from the *Muso*. However, if the chicken escapes, the witch is then delivered from the *Muso*.

However, it is commonplace in both Kom and Venda that purchased witchcraft can get out of control. The transference of witchcraft techniques may not be compatible with one's personality. This may render the purchaser insane, with constant hallucinations. The following case from Kom demonstrates a witchcraft transaction that went totally out of control.

Case 3, Salitoto: Witchcraft transaction that goes horribly wrong in Kom

His real name was Genesis Alo-oh. He came from Aboh. He was nicknamed Salitoto because of his evil deeds. Salitoto started by distributing witchcraft medicine in Aboh. This led to the killing of a herdsman, Hamidou Abdou, who belonged to the Fulani people. Salitoto then passed the medicine to one lady who in turn killed her boyfriend. The villagers learnt of his deeds from his hallucinations. He would wander around villages and swear during social gatherings that he had sold medicine to a lady who refused to pay him. He would disclose names of people who came to him to learn how to kill those they hated. As a result, Salitoto was banished from Aboh and had to seek refuge in Fundong.

In Fundong, Salitoto was carefully monitored by fellow villagers so that he could not distribute medicines again. One night, he was followed by his monitors after leaving the house with two bottles of medicine. The monitors caught him handing one of the bottles to a man from another village. Salitoto was immediately brought before the traditional council in Fundong. Here he disclosed that he had given his medicines to seven people in Fundong. Two of the people he mentioned confessed that they used his medicines to kill fellow villagers. They achieved this by putting the medicine into traditional beer. As a result of this, the number of monitors was increased to have people who would also look after him at night.

Salitoto's hallucinations became more elaborate. He would not only disclose the names of the people he helped get killed, but he would also repeatedly call out the name of the person who taught him these medicines. He revealed that he got his medicines from one Maling Ibua from Buh village in Menchum Division; that he bought these medicines at a huge price but the medicines were now bothering him; he would like to return the medicines but does not know where to find Ibua since he is a wanderer. When fieldwork in Kom was finished, Salitoto was ordered to sleep or spend the nights in Laikom, since it is on the mountain and a distance from villagers' compounds.

Witchcraft Techniques

In both Kom and Venda, witches receive medicines through incisions under their tongues, usually before adolescence. This enables them to possess the power of the tongue: if a witch curses one in anger, then something bad is bound to happen to one. Most witches, however, back up their words with a witchcraft action. They make sure that their curse materialises by employing various witchcraft techniques as reflected below.

Tshiliso/si lufa djem

Witches in Venda employ a technique called *tshiliso*, known as *si luf a djem* in Kom. Through this technique, a victim of witchcraft is made to swallow an object – usually a piece of meat mixed with magical powders – which on reaching the stomach changes into a living organism or object that controls the functioning of the body. The most common form of control is the object's ability to tamper

40

with the victim's respiratory system. After establishing itself in the body, this object may show itself as an itchy skin rash, referred to by the Vhavenda as *mulilo* (Mabogo, 1990:35).

The Vhavenda believe that a person has *nowa* – a central organ in the body possibly located in or very close to the stomach – which controls the whole functioning of the body. Witches have expertise on how the *nowa* functions, and they use *tshiliso* to annex it in different ways. Once the *nowa* has swallowed the magical object, it starts to behave under its influence. A person bewitched in this way cannot be treated successfully as he or she vomits the medicines (ibid:35).

Treatment of *tshiliso* involves *tshivholovholo* – an application of medicines that intoxicate the *nowa* to allow for treatment or that affect the *nowa* in such a way that it returns to normal functioning. Traditional healers treat this by cooking medicines in a pot. The medicine pot is then removed from the fire and placed in front of the patient, who is seated on a small stool astride the steaming pot. A thick blanket is thrown over both the patient and the pot. A patient is held down to ensure that he or she does not escape from the choking and overpowering steam. When the blanket is removed, the patient is drenched in perspiration.

Si luf a djem is considered a new form of witchcraft in Kom. Unlike in Venda, this form of witchcraft cannot be cured by *ngambe*. The cure is instead revealed to the victim in a dream. Victims dream of a certain herb, which the *ngambe* later refers to as a cure.

In treating this form of witchcraft in both Kom and Venda, certain rituals are carried out to ensure that the victim responds positively to the treatment. This ritual is referred to as *chiti* (forgive) the victim in Kom. In Venda, it is called *u swikiswa kha vhafhasi* (to deliver to the ancestors).

U shelela/lef

Another form of witchcraft technique that involves swallowing is *u shelela* in Venda. This is the most popular and feared technique since it is done usually during the day and at social gatherings. Poison is put into another person's food or drink. The common poison amongst the Vhavenda is *tshiganame*, which involves the application of dry crocodile's brains into a drink of the victim. The brains are scraped under the fingernail and then the tip of the finger is dipped into the cup of a victim. Once swallowed in a drink, the victim dies instantly from uncontrollable vomiting of blood.

As a form of containing this type of witchcraft, a person who kills a crocodile in Venda is expected to burn it. Even though the Vhavenda often claim there are ways and medicines with which to treat victims of this technique, such claims are never substantiated. One neither hears of nor comes across a victim who survived *tshiganame*. The Vhavenda attribute this lack of survivors to the unavailability of healers on the scene who can immediately treat the victim once the poison is diagnosed.

The Kom version of *u shelela* is *lef*, a technique that involves adding poison into kolanuts, food or drinks. The two common poisons are *ngvim* (the bile of a python) and *ambol andim* (brains of a hairy frog). Once swallowed in a drink, these poisons lead to destruction of the digestive system. Victims of the poisons die instantly and from excessive vomiting of blood. There is a third type of poison that involves the whiskers of a leopard. When poisoned, the victim only lives for a maximum of three days. This kind of *lef* leads to a whopping cough. If the poison is immediately diagnosed, a *ngambe* may cure the victim by giving him or her a concoction of boiled herbs to drink or a medicinal paste to eat. Unlike in Venda, some victims of *lef* survive to tell their stories.

Owing to their knowledge of *lef*, the Kom people demand that any person who kills a python or leopard should take the bile or whiskers to the chief. The python also has to be skinned by fellow villagers. This action safeguards the killer against mistrust or suspicion by fellow villagers if someone dies from the effect of poisoning. A person who skins the python alone or is found to be in possession of a leopard's head may be ostracised or exiled.

To minimise the risk of people being poisoned through *lef* and *u shelela* in Kom and Venda respectively, people are not encouraged to serve others a drink without first taking a sip. This custom is emphasised in social gatherings as it is believed that such occasions

42

are often used for nefarious activities. The act of sipping is, in Venda, referred to as *u ntsha mushonga*: to remove the medicine, that is *chu mulu* in Kom.

U livhanya/si ling

There is *si ling* in Kom, a technique that involves magical performances that are performed by witches to get those they dislike into trouble. Vhavenda call this technique *u livhanya*. Witches are said to use their supernatural powers to cast a spell on their victims so that they experience endless misfortunes. People who suffer from *u livhanya* or *si ling* are usually the object of intense dislike, which is usually accompanied by rage with an intention to kill by their assailants. Victims of this technique may be mugged, beaten up for crimes they have not committed or be made to get involved in car accidents. The chain of misfortunes may eventually be fatal if the spell is not reversed.

It is also believed in Kom and Venda that witches sprinkle their medicines at night around the fireplace of those they hate. The targeted victims unknowingly burn the invisible medicines and inhale the smoke, the result of which is that the targeted family members are constantly involved in a quarrel and never know peace. Witches may also remove little amounts of ashes from the fireplace of their victims so they could 'work' it with their medicines in order to produce harmful results to their victims. It is for this reason that it is customary in both Kom and Venda to clean the fireplace before and immediately after making fire.

Owing to their understanding of *u livhanya* or *si ling* – that witches possess the supernatural powers to cast a spell on people who are travelling so that misfortunes may coincide with their journey – parents and children in both societies agree on a non-disclosure policy of place and time of their movements. When travelling, parents often do not tell their children the exact place and time of their journey. In the event the children are told, this is done with a strict instruction that they should keep it a secret or mention a different place when asked. It is argued that this is necessary in order to protect the travelling parents from the harmful actions of witches.

43

The two cases that follow will demonstrate how, as a result of a witchcraft belief, people in Kom and Venda resort in similar behaviour that an outsider may find hard to understand. Mmbangiseni – my gatekeeper in the Makuya area in Venda – narrated the first case after we had a very difficult encounter with Mphando, a traditional healer. For two weeks we had been visiting Mphando's house without luck. His daughters kept telling us that we had just missed him and advised that we should return the following day. It was only after three weeks that Mphando returned home. During a meeting with him, Mphando told us that his daughters knew that he was away and that he would return after two weeks. For us, it was hard to accept that his daughters watched us almost every day for two weeks travelling more than 45 kilometres to their house while they had this knowledge.

Case 4: Non-disclosure as protection against *u livhanya* and *si ling* in Venda and Kom

"My sisters and I were raised by a single parent – our mother – since our father was a migrant worker in the city. Our mother would not tell us exactly when our father would be returning home during the festive season. At times she would even lie and tell us that our father was not coming back that particular Christmas. Once our father was home, neither he nor our mother would tell us his exact date of departure to the city. If they told us, which was rare, they did so with a strict instruction that we were not to disclose these dates to anyone, not even our friends. The reason for this, we were told, was to protect our father from witchcraft. We were also told that this explained why our friends would not tell us when and to where their parents were travelling. Indeed, we were very loyal to one another as children, but the information we passed onto one another regarding the itineraries of our parents was often misleading. Such is the world that we live in. If you are lucky and exceptional, I will tell you I will not be around but do not expect information on where and when I will be going."

The Cameroon case I encountered involves a medical doctor by profession, her children and workers. The doctor had businesses running in three different places in Cameroon. From time to time, she would travel in and out of the country. Her children were the first to know about her journey since she was staying with all of them. She would also check on her workers in different parts of the country before she left, even though she would not disclose when she would be out of the country except to say she should not be expected in the area since she would be preoccupied with other duties. I had an opportunity to work with this doctor for months. It was during this period that I learnt that she would be travelling to France for a week's conference. This I assumed her family was aware of, even her workers since we visited them a day before she was due to travel. Two days after her departure, I had a meeting with one of her workers, the very worker with whom she met a day before she left. To my surprise, the worker advised me that if I needed his boss, I should call her house and not the office since she indicated she would not be coming until further notice. I advised the worker that his employer was out of the country, and therefore I was not going to call her house. He was not surprised except to say that it was typical of her and that he suspected the moment she asked him if there was anything that would be needed in the following few weeks since she would be working from home. "It is because of the issue [witchcraft] that you are researching that people don't tell the exact time and place of their movement," the worker further explains. Five days later, I met the doctor's daughter. We were talking about her mother and she was surprised I knew when her mother would be returning from abroad. She was told that her mother was visiting Germany and not France. I was astonished by her contentment and immediate defence that her mother lied to her for a good cause, and that this was something that every parent was doing. This immediately reminded me of Mphando's daughters and the story that Mmbangiseni narrated to me back in Venda.

Afu a lemna/tshipfula

In Kom and Venda, witches are believed to have the expertise to indirectly bewitch their victims by using their belongings as objects of bewitchment. This technique is called *afu a lemna*. In Venda, it is called *tshipfula* or *u doba*. It is a magical practice in which a person is bewitched by making use of the soil with one's footprint or samples of one's hair, nail or clothing and discharges from the body such as sweat, urine or faeces. For example, witches may take one's clothing and wash it so they can take the dirt that remains in the water. They use the dirt to negatively influence the well-being of their victim. Witches also use this technique to destroy their victims' wealth. They would, out of jealousy or hatred of those whose cattle have a high reproductive rate, mix their medicines with cattle manure to reduce fecundity. This mixture is woven to form a ring-like structure that is placed vertically between two stones.

Witches are known to sprinkle medicines across the path that is frequently used by their victims. They may also apply medicines to a stick or thread and place it across the path. Upon touching or stepping on the medicines, the victim may start developing an incurable cancer. Ritual performances and incantations accompany the application of medicines by the witch to ensure that the medicines affect the targeted person and not anyone else who uses the path. The ritual involves the calling of the victim's name and invoking his or her ancestors. In order to get such intimate information about their victims, witches are believed to work in collusion with some of the victim's relatives. Such is the ambiguity with witch relatives are viewed in these societies. While one's relatives may symbolise available support for one in times of need, they may also constitute one's Achilles heel that can be exploited by witches.

Certain measures are taken in both societies in order to counter *afu a lemna* or *tshipfula*. New possessions such as cars and residences are introduced to a healer to protect them with medicines so that witches do not use them to bewitch the owner. In addition, the ancestors are informed of new acquisitions and kindly requested to protect them from the destructive actions of witches. "Ancestor spirits who normally protect the family left on earth can withdraw

46

this protection if upset by a living member of the clan... They must be appeased continually, especially in troubled times, lest they be angered through neglect and jealousy or slighted by broken religious tenets" (Holland, 2002:8).

Ndadzi (lightning)

In Venda, there is a feared witchcraft technique called *Ndadzi*. It is believed that some witches have the supernatural powers to cause lightning to kill their victims or destroy their property. In addition to natural lightning, it is understood that there is a lightning that is caused by male witches, which can be prevented by getting protection from traditional healers. It is for this reason that when lightning strikes the Muvenda always suspect that there could be some individuals out there who have tampered with natural forces. After causing lightning a witch is believed to go to the nearest river to wash off the medicines: *ndadzi ya rwa hu gidimelwa mulamboni*: once lightning strikes people rush to the river, so goes the Tshivenda saying. Due to the fact that this kind of technique is associated with male witches, people often monitor that part of a river which is used by men. Such a rush may help people catch the culprit while still naked and washing off the medicines.

In Kom, there also exists an awareness of the other form of lightning in addition to the natural one. This kind of lightning is however not associated with witches but with certain traditional healers who send it only at the request of those who feel wronged. Unlike in Venda where lightning is used for evil ends, in Kom lightning is used as a form of retributive justice, particularly against those who borrow other people's property and never bother to return it. Lightning is also believed to strike those who have not appeased their ancestors. If a person, out of jealousy, approaches a specialist to send lightning to strike someone innocent, and the person is not a wrongdoer, lightning will somehow miss the intended victim and come back to strike the jealous person. Hence before the Kom specialist sends lightning, certain rituals are conducted to ascertain the validity of the case before hand, that is to find out if the intended victim is the real wrongdoer. It is this notion of retributive justice

47

that lightning is associated with that prevents people who die from lightning strikes from being laid in state, not even for a day or night, before burial. Their deaths are considered to be an abomination to the land, and therefore their corpses are given an instant burial, and always at night[14].

Case 5: Lightning strike at Mandiwana village in Venda

Maluta was a businessman who owned taxis. In 1983, he was staying at Mandiwana village and his homestead was neighbouring those of Ramabulana and Tshilata. Maluta was well respected in the community, despite the fact that he was frequently involved in taxi disputes with other taxi owners in several areas of Venda. One Friday afternoon, it started raining heavily with thunder. After a while, Ndiambani – Ramabulana's son who was playing outside the house – started screaming while pointing at a bird that was hanging in the sky. He was heard by the boys who were outside Maluta's house. Together they watched the bird land on top of Tshilata's mud-hut. Suddenly there was a lightning strike and Tshilata's mud-hut was on fire. The boys then watched the bird flying towards the direction of Nzhelele River. They alerted the adults, who braved the rain and ran towards the river.

On approaching the river, community members found a naked man standing in the river. On seeing them, the naked man raised his arm, and lightning was emitted from his armpit. This brought down those who were in the front row. However, villagers were arriving in large numbers from both sides of the river. With no more lightning to emit from his armpits, the man pleaded for mercy from the charging villagers. He stated that he was from Sinthumule village – approximately 100 kilometres away from Mandiwana village. One taxi man hired him to kill Maluta who was alleged to be a problem in the

---

[14] Also deaths resulting from certain sicknesses were considered abomination in West African societies. In his novel of the Igbo tribe in Nigeria, Chinua Achebe (1958:13) wrote, "when a man was afflicted with swelling in the stomach and the limbs he was not allowed to die in the house. He was carried to the Evil Forest and left there to die.

taxi industry. He indicated that while in the vicinity he could not see the homestead of Maluta (the invisibility was attributed to the fact that Maluta's homestead was protected by a healer). Realizing that he was running out of time, the man decided to land on Tshilata's homestead. He indicated that he was very sorry and that he never intended to inflict harm on the Tshilata family. After this confession, one of the villagers axed him to death. The following weekend, during a meeting of the traditional council, a resolution was taken that every adult villager should contribute R1. Once all the money was collected, senior elders were sent to find a reputable healer who could 'protect' the whole village against future lightning attacks.

Conclusion

The description of witchcraft beliefs and practices in both Kom and Venda as presented in this chapter demonstrate that despite the use of the expression "African witchcraft" to refer to witchcraft beliefs and practices that are found in various localities in the African continent, these beliefs are neither wholly homogeneous nor coherent. Witchcraft beliefs and practices on the continent vary from one locality to another. The cases presented illustrate that in the world of most Africans there are occurrences that confirm the existence of witchcraft. Not only does witchcraft shed light into people's reactions to life's challenges but it also provides an understanding of people's actions that would otherwise look insane or archaic. It is this subjective reality of witchcraft and its management – both at local and national levels – as opposed to whether witchcraft exists or not, on which the focus of research and policy should be. The next chapter will illustrate various measures put in place by villagers, at family and community levels, in their daily efforts to counter this occult force.

Chapter Three

Containment of Witchcraft at Family and Community Levels

Introduction

Africans believe that they can influence how the environment affects them, because they believe that the effect of the environment on particular lives is conditioned by the actions of other people, particularly evil people such as witches and sorcerers. Thus, Africans see their problems as deriving from their failure to control ...other people. Such control involves an attempt to identify other peoples' intentions and dispositions (Karp, 1995:217).

In Africa, it is idle to begin with the question whether witches exist or not. For most here the concern is not about that; rather they are concerned about how to combat these witches (Bola, 1973:175).

Witchcraft containment is part of the daily efforts in Kom and Venda to control and domesticate the actions of other people. The containment has always taken the form of protection at the family and community levels. Regrettably, for many decades the containment of witchcraft has been largely ignored in the literature on African witchcraft. This is despite the fact that such work may provide a plausible explanation in the understanding of witchcraft violence and its variation over time within a given society. It may also help in understanding the variation in witchcraft violence amongst African societies. For instance in this case, why is it that despite its prevalence in both societies, witchcraft does not lead to open violence in Kom, while in Venda such violence is commonplace?

It is only recently that containment, and not suppression, of witchcraft has become both the subject of research amongst social scientists and a policy issue with which postcolonial African decision-makers are concerned. As Ciekawy and Geschiere (1998:6) remark, "witchcraft's capacity for a continual increase of scale is met by people's equally avid search for new means to contain it." In her contribution, Meyer (1998) shows how Pentecontalists, in contrast to the official churches in Ghana recognize witchcraft as a reality and succeed in combating it. Amongst the Kom and the Vhavenda, there are institutions that detect, disable and punish witches. It is this form of containment that occurs at both family and community levels that this chapter concerns itself with.

Family containment of witchcraft

The modern Kom and Venda societies still bear the characteristics of a traditional society. They remain simple and communalistic. They retain both the nuclear and extended family as the essence of human organization and provision. Low levels of conflict in these communities have their roots in the custom of encouraging and using a family as a primary institution of conflict resolution. Witchcraft is one of the phenomena that are usually sources of conflict in these societies, and the family as an institution has devised several ways of not only resolving these conflicts but also preventing them.

The family is therefore the primary institution where the battle against witchcraft – prevention and combating – is waged, and traditional healers play a central role in this regard. Compared to their counterparts in modern medicine, traditional healers specialise in traditional medicine. They enjoy clairvoyant powers and have a more spiritual aura. They have the ability to detect witchcraft, and use ancestral or supernatural authority for their healing powers (Tebbe, 2007).

Doctoring of a homestead

The doctoring of a homestead is a common feature in Kom and Venda. A traditional healer is consulted to protect people and their property against all forms of witchcraft. While the protection of family members is performed at any time, the doctoring of homesteads is done only at night. Very few healers are specialists in this area. In both societies, healers from places afar are preferred when it comes to family protection.

In Venda, the protection is believed to disarm witches. It denies witches access to a homestead. It makes witches forget their targets, lose their way, be gripped with fear, lose courage, or forget their purpose once they have entered a homestead. Witches who are members of a homestead are made to oversleep. Some homesteads are protected in such a way that witches may enter a homestead but may neither complete their task nor leave the premises (Mabogo, 1990). *Mutavhatsindi (Brackenridgea zanguebarica)* is a popularly known plant species used in the doctoring of people, houses and villages against witchcraft attacks. It is believed that a homestead that is protected by a traditional healer using *mutavhatsindi* is immune from lightning strikes and attacks of witches.

In Kom, some anti-witchcraft medicines can have a deadly effect on the witch and his or her family. The medicines, when planted, function as a magnet: a witch who crosses over them carries home an illness and if not treated by a healer, the witch may die. Other anti-witchcraft medicines immobilize a witch so that he or she remains on the spot of bewitchment and can only be freed by the healer who planted such medicines. The healer does this by applying certain medicines on the body of such a witch. A paste produced with castor oil is popularly rubbed on the doors of compounds to repel witches. The paste is also placed in a compound inside a container that is kept open in order for the paste to be effective.

Protection of family members

It is widely accepted throughout Africa that everyone runs the risk of being harmed by a witch: sooner or later, the evil is likely to get you. You arm yourself with protective medicine, hoping this will ward off danger but knowing that it sometimes fails (Holland, 2001:10).

The protection against witchcraft attack in Venda and Kom does not end with the doctoring of a homestead, but is also extended to members within such a homestead. At birth, an infant undergoes what in Venda is called *u thuswa* within its first year. This treatment is performed on an infant with medicines to immunize it against evil magical influences. A healer performs the treatment before the child is allowed to leave the hut (Van Warmelo, 1989:380). The protection involves the blending of medicine with a razor blade and introducing it into the child's system. In addition, a medicinal ring may be tied around the child's waist. It is believed a child who is well protected is immune to most witchcraft attacks, which would otherwise be harmful or fatal to someone not protected. When attacked by witches, such a child (even an adult) would fail to fall into a deep sleep. If such a child or an adult was already in deep sleep, he or she would suddenly wake up. Owing to the protection of *mutavhatsindi*, the Vhatavhatsindi – a clan group that calls itself after the plant – are believed to be invincible against attacks of ritual murderers. The plant either blinds or causes ritual murderers to quarrel amongst themselves, therefore rendering them unable to attack their target. This is done to guard against a risk that a local healer could become corruptible and divulge the protective medicines to local witches, and thus rendering the homestead vulnerable.

For witches to succeed in breaking the protection of certain medicines, they need to know the types of medicines involved in the *u thuswa* of their victims. They obtain this information from the next-of-kin of their victim. The relative becomes the main contact and helps clear the way by divulging which medicines have been used to protect the victim. Witches use this information to get access to the marked victim. If the relative refuses to grant witches access, it is believed that witches can do no harm to the victim. *Uyo thoho yawe i a konda*: that one's head is difficult, so goes the Tshivenda saying. This refers to people who are well protected by medicines to an extent that witches find them hard to break. Such people usually fight and call voicelessly during a subconscious state in their sleep. This is called *tshitsikeledzi*. When one has *tshitsikeledzi*, it is said witches were around and wanted to bewitch one. However owing to one's protection, witches find this difficult. Thus begins their efforts to force one into deep sleep.

54

In Kom, this type of witchcraft is associated with the *wul ntuh*. These are the witches who when they want to hurt their victim, hold part of their own bodies and call the victim's name. They stand aside and act in shock waves and the victim feels the pain. When a victim discovers he or she is being beaten by a *wul ntuh*, the victim removes medicines from the barn and burns them in the hearth. The resultant smoke repels witches. There are certain protected homesteads in Kom that no *wul ntuh* can tamper with. If the *wul ntuh* forces entry then he or she would die. Before dying the *wul ntuh* confesses where he or she was caught by medicines.

The above are some of the tireless efforts that people and families in Kom and Venda make in their daily struggle against the ever-threatening force of witchcraft. For one to successfully protect oneself against a witchcraft attack, many factors work in combination. What follows below is a case I encountered during fieldwork in Venda which involved a family combating a persistent witchcraft attack.

Case 6, Khathu Maila: Family containment of witchcraft from outside, in Venda

In 1997, Khathu Maila, a young man of 20 years of age was in a love relationship with Mashudu Denga, a young woman of 18 years of age. The Denga family was known to possess inherited witchcraft that involved a *tokotoshi* in the act of bewitching. Things went wrong in 1998 when Mashudu fell pregnant. The pregnancy was reported to Khathu's family. Khathu denied that he was responsible, and claimed that Mashudu was involved in another love affair with a young man from another village. On hearing Khathu's denial, Mashudu's grandmother stated that there was nothing that could be done to make Khathu accept his deeds, and thanked the Maila family for their audience. When Mashudu's grandmother left the Maila homestead, she looked at Khathu and said "we will sort the matter out ourselves, *u do zwivhona*: you shall see.

After the Denga delegation had left, Khathu's grandmother told other family members that she feared for her grandson's life. She indicated that the last words uttered by Mashudu's grandmother were threatening considering the history of witchcraft in the Denga family[15]. Three months later, Khathu told his brother, Hudzani, that he heard voices calling his name while he was sleeping. Hudzani dismissed Khathu and suggested that he could have been dreaming. As the voice persisted, the two brothers informed their grandmother about this weird incident, who advised that they should wait and see how things developed.

A month later when the two brothers were sleeping in their hut, Khathu woke up and lit the candle, and was foaming at the mouth. The following week Khathu was woken from a deep-sleep by a voice that resembled his mother's. While he was still numb from shock, Khathu could feel the part of the blanket covering his head being removed. Khathu then moved his right hand to the side of his head to catch whatever was uncovering his face. His hand landed on the hairy leg of something that felt like an animal. A tug-of-war ensued in darkness, and Khathu screamed for his bother Hudzani, who was sleeping in the same hut. When Hudzani responded, the animal scratched the back of Khathu's right hand, and suddenly Khathu released the creature. By the time Hudzani lit the lamp, the creature had vanished into darkness. With Khathu's hand bleeding, the brothers went to another hut to wake up their grandmother, who advised them not to put the lamp out until dawn.

Two days later, Khathu fell ill. He eventually stopped going to school at the end of March 1999. Khathu's illness worsened and he started hallucinating. He frequently started just disappearing, leaving his home in the morning and returning at night. This started to bother his grandmother since nobody knew where Khathu was spending his days. In April, Khathu failed to return home. Hudzani and other brothers from the extended families went in search of Khathu and found him by the riverside on the third day. Khathu

---

[15] Amongst the Vhavenda, it is believed that when one of the feuding parties utters the words u do zwivhona, one acknowledges that the matter has not been resolved amicably and that one implies that one threatens to deal with the issue in a way that may harm the other, and this is usually through witchcraft.

complained of something in his throat that was tampering with his breathing.

Khathu was taken to Musweswe, a well-renowned healer in the village. After throwing the divination set, Musweswe indicated that Khathu had been inflicted with *tshipengo*, a technique used by *vhaloi* to de-humanize their victims by driving them mad. Khathu had been forced to swallow some magical powders while in his sleep and these powders had annexed Khathu's *nowa* (abdominal organs). Khathu was therefore no longer in control of his life since he was acting under the influence of witchcraft. Musweswe attributed Khathu's breathing difficulties to the magical powders that he was made to swallow by a *tokoloshi* in his sleep. The *tokoloshi* was the creature that Khathu had fought against the other night. The voices that Khathu was hearing were those of his mother's ancestors. They were waking him up so as to protect him from the attack of witches.[16] It was because of these ancestors that Khathu was still alive. Musweswe revealed that the people who were behind Khathu's illness were determined to take his life.

Before Musweswe performed any treatment she threw down the divination set to ascertain Khathu's fate. Each time Musweswe threw down the divination set, they repeatedly brought similar combinations. These were *thwalima* and *mufhirifhiri*.[17] Musweswe interpreted this to mean that there was no certainty as to the outcome of the treatment: during treatment the magical object could succumb to the pressure and Khathu may be able to breathe well again, or the object may overpower the treatment, block Khathu's respiratory system and kill him instantly. One thing was certain though: if such treatment was not conducted Khathu would eventually die. Khathu's grandmother then decided that the treatment should take place. The treatment involved a technique of healing called *tshivholovholo*. This

---

[16] Witches call one with the intention that if one answers one would then fall victim to their bewitchment. Achebe (1958:29) stated, "when people [in Nigeria] answered calls from outside in the night, they would call back "that is me." They never answered yes in fear it might be an evil spirit calling."

[17] *Thwalima* symbolises danger, fire, conflict or bloodshed. *Mufhirifhiri* symbolises trouble, unrest or chaos in the family (Stayt, 1932: 288).

involves placing the patient in a tent of blankets that is covering continually boiling water. Around this tent are usually three to four people who ensure that air is not getting through. Next to the tent are red-hot stones in a fire. The healer takes each of these stones and places them in a pot of boiling water together with some medicines for the patient to inhale the steam. It is believed this intoxicates the nowa of the patient and allows for treatment, or affects it in such a way that it returns to normal functioning.

Khathu survived the treatment and gradually began breathing normally. The following month, Khathu started hallucinating and showing signs of insanity. One day he was almost run over by a truck, and had his right hand broken. Khathu was taken to Musweswe again. She stated that on realizing that Khathu had survived *tshipengo* and a breathing problem, the witches wanted to kill him with *u livhanya,* a technique that is employed by witches to bring about an effect that the victim appears to have met with an accident. She indicated that Khathu could be healed only if the act was directed back to the witches. She advised Khathu's grandmother to consult Muedi, a male healer in Maelula, a village which was about 100 kilometres away.

Khathu was taken to Muedi in July, who on seeing him confirmed the problem as diagnosed by Musweswe. He revealed that Khathu was infected with *thuri* that were given a clear message by their witch master that they should come back with the victim[18]. Khathu's grandmother was then asked to leave Khathu behind until he was cured. Muedi promised Khathu's grandmother that he would return the witchcraft to the owner, and that the culprit would die in a car accident. That would mark the end of Khathu's misery because this would even scare other witches with whom the main witch was collaborating. In January 2000, Khathu's family learnt that there was someone who had been run down by a car. This was the

---

[18] This witchcraft attack was intended to kill its victim, rather than to traumatise him with illness. Unlike the witchcraft attacks that inflict suffering, this one that is meant to cause death is more persistent and resistant to treatment, and may when exorcised be fatal to its master or his or her family.

grandmother of Mashudu Denga, the girl Khathu was alleged to have impregnated. Khathu suddenly regained sanity and was returned home in February.

The above case emphasizes the form of witchcraft containment found at the family level. This form of containment is covert in that only the bewitched and his or her family are engaged in a supernatural battle against the witch. Once the bewitched decides to combat witchcraft in this way, any physical confrontation with the witch is ruled out. A healer becomes central to such a spiritual tug of war. He or she allays the fear of witchcraft attack that the bewitched may have.

The case demonstrates that witches are industrious strategists that apply various techniques in their effort to inflict harm on their victims. Against Khathu, techniques like *tshiliso, tshipengo* and *u livhanya* were used in an effort to kill him. This however does not render the Maila family helpless. In response, the family relentlessly combats witchcraft and ever decides to have it returned to the owner with deadly consequences.

Muedi's decision to send the witchcraft back to Mashudu's grandmother reveals the dual role that traditional healers may play in witchcraft matters. A healer may have the ability to apply curative medicine or use certain techniques to destroy or inflict serious harm on others. "This is the traditional healer through whose spirit justice is restored. If someone in the community wrongs the other...and the victim is unable to obtain redress through legal channels, he [she] can seek a medium with the power to punish the guilty party by inflicting madness, illness or death on successive family members (Holland, 2001:13)."

Khathu's resistance to several witchcraft attacks speaks volumes of the well-being of his family despite the vulnerability of their homestead. It indicates what the Vhavenda would call *mudi u a leluwa*: the homestead is light. This refers to a homestead that is relatively vulnerable against the attacks of witches. In this case, witches gained access into the Maila homestead several times as they were able to employ various witchcraft techniques. However, Khathu's resistance to all these techniques shows that individually, his family members are well protected.

The intervention of the Maila ancestors to save their grandson is a sign that the witchcraft attack occurred at a time when the Maila family had appeased its ancestors. Appeasing the ancestors and keeping the relatives happy is very important in Kom and Venda as it is believed that when witches fail on several attempts to bewitch or kill someone, they usually contact a relative of such a victim so that he or she can reveal the medicine used to protect the victim. This is referred by the Vhavenda as *u vula ndila*: to open the way. A relative may also tell witches the name of the ancestor who has been ignored by the victim's family.

In Kom, witches use their medicines to invoke the *nkfe nse* (ghost) of the family. The *nkfe nse* is a deceased relative whose burial rites – feathering of fowls and slaughtering of a goat by men and the offering of corn and beans by women – have been neglected by the living relatives. When a person dies, these rites must be performed to ensure that the deceased family member has a peaceful and safe journey to the world of ancestors. When the *nkfe nse* is invoked any witchcraft that comes the victim's way is covered by *nkfe nse*, thus making it hard to diagnose the illness. This eventually leads to the death of the victim, while his or her next-of-kin look for the correct diagnosis. Healers are able to unveil the witchcraft behind the *nkfe nse* through their divination set using *ndong*[19]. They shake the *ndong* which may either remain silent or produce a sound. This helps identify a deceased relative who is covering the witchcraft and the kind of sacrifice required in order to put to rest this ancestor.

The case also demonstrates that traditional healers play a pivotal role in the combating of witchcraft at a family level. They protect family members from and fortify homesteads against witchcraft attacks. In addition, they detect, disable and punish witches. They play a prominent role in relating and interpreting that which is beyond access by 'ordinary

---

[19] Horn of a goat with certain small nuts inside.

people'.[20] As shown above, each time the Maila family were confronted with a different witchcraft attack, it was Musweswe's task to interpret and explain such supernatural events, diagnose the sickness, identify the witch behind the attack, find the cure or refer Khathu to a relevant specialist for treatment. This role of healers is crucial in that it provides a sense of security to villagers against attack from occult forces. It is a regulatory mechanism that ensures that the accuser deals with the accused through a healer. Direct confrontation between the accuser and the accused is avoided, thereby preventing an explosive situation.

Successful combating of witchcraft however does not happen at all times. When the bewitched exhaust all means of protection against a persistent witchcraft attack, there is likelihood that accusations may arise. After one or two successful acts of protection, the victim may, on losing the battle, decide to confront the witch or spread accusations with the hope that this will scare the alleged witch and bring the witchcraft attack to an end. The recommended alternative is for the victim to appeal to a traditional council to intervene. Equally the alleged witch may, upon being confronted, decide to report the matter to the traditional council. As it shall become evident, unlike in Kom, this option was legally taken away in Venda.

Community containment of witchcraft

Traditional authorities are still the main structures that people rely on for support and most services at local level in many rural and semi-rural areas in both Cameroon and South Africa. Their primary function is to regulate and control relationships and social behaviour within a traditional community. They are in essence people-oriented and therefore ensure social cohesion, security, peace and stability in their communities. Traditional communities also have an indigenous legal system that applies indigenous law with the full participation of all stakeholders (Donkers & Murray, 1997:42). Witchcraft matters are

---

[20] Amongst the Vhavenda, the use of the term 'ordinary people' is contextual. It may refer to poor people, or as in this instance, it can refer to all people who are not specialists in traditional medicine.

also dealt with under such law. On witchcraft cases, a platform for arbitration and conciliation is provided for in the traditional councils. It is on this basis that traditional councils have relative success in dealing with witchcraft disputes.

Combating witchcraft at village level in Venda

In Venda, I attended the fortnightly meetings of a *khoro* (traditional council) at Mandiwana village. I was also able to observe members of *Khoro Tshitumbe* (Executive Council) presiding over sensitive cases such as adultery, threats to individuals, land disputes, child and women abuse, child bearing and parenting. The cases used to include those of witchcraft but this is no longer the case as it is considered illegal.

I had discussions for five days with four members of *Khoro Tshitumbe* who differed according to their positions. They were two males and two females. One male member was the *mukoma*, that is the chief's representative and has been serving in this position since 1941. There is hardly any crisis that occurs in the village without it being brought to the attention of the *mukoma*. The other male member was the *maine*, that is the village healer. The *maine* is the one who ensures that the village is 'protected' against lightning during rainy seasons. He also 'protects' *khoro* from the magical influences of witches. The two females were the *makhadzi* and *mukoma*. The *makhadzi* is the title given to the sister of the chief in the village. She had extensive knowledge of most of the activities that happened in the village, from circumcision rites to cases that were brought before *khoro*. The other female was a *mukoma* whose functions are similar to those of the male *mukoma*. She however resided on the other corner of the village.

The commonality among the four people was that they had been living in and serving the village for a long time. They all served under the reign of at least two chiefs in succession. Amongst other things, we talked about different cases in detail (most of which had been documented in the old book of *khoro*), the transformation that had taken place in *dzikhoro* over the decades, and the changes that had taken place in the handling of witchcraft cases.

They stated that when they used to mediate in witchcraft cases, there was less violence than that witnessed in the 1980s in Venda. The matter would be reported to the *mukoma* by one of the feuding parties (the accuser or accused). The *mukoma* would brief the chief about the matter before a date was set on which *Khoro Tshitumbe* was convened. Both the accuser/s and the accused were requested to tell their stories and, where possible, bring witnesses to support them. They were also allowed to cross-examine each other. Once the *Khoro Tshitumbe* had taken a decision, the feuding parties were informed of the outcome. Both parties would be warned that they would be presumed responsible for any bad thing that could happen to either of them. This warning was meant to prevent either of the two parties from harming the other, directly or indirectly.

Not all cases that came before the members of *Khoro Tshitumbe* were peacefully resolved. Some decisions of the *Khoro Tshitumbe* would be contested by one of the feuding parties, and these would be referred to the council of village elders for advice. If still unresolved the case would be referred to the Mphephu Tribal Authority, which is a *khoro* consisting of chiefs of different villages within the jurisdiction of a paramount chief. This procedure of addressing disputes is still followed on all cases except those of witchcraft. When villagers report witchcraft cases to traditional councils, they are turned back and reminded that the law no longer allows such matters to be handled at this level. At the meeting I attended of the Mphephu Tribal Authority, I was told that its members no longer considered witchcraft disputes and that the Tribal Authority had actually issued a notice to all traditional councils under it informing them that they should no longer refer such cases for its attention.

However, one chief, a member of the Tribal Authority, confidently indicated to me that at the village level, some chiefs would from time to time intervene in witchcraft matters in order to save the lives of those accused. He narrated the following case to me.

63

Case 7: A witch tries to turn Matunde into a zombie

In a village next to the Beitbridge Border Post, a 12 year old boy called Matunde went missing and was immediately reported to the tribal authority. An emergency meeting was called in which the chief informed the villagers about the sad development. A decision was then taken that a search team should be formed with the task of finding the missing child.

The first day went by and the search yielded no results. On the second day, shepherds reported to the chief that they encountered Matunde during the day while busy in the bush. They claimed that they attempted to approach Matunde but he ran so fast and tirelessly that they could not keep pace. He then disappeared into bushes.

The chief again requested that there be an emergency meeting of the community to allow the shepherds an opportunity to explain what they had seen. After the shepherds' narration, the community decided that a further search should be conducted for the missing boy despite the fact that it was already late. Once again the search did not yield any positive outcome.

The community leaders then decided that the search should continue into the third day. The search resumed in the morning until lunch time without success. Around the same place where the shepherds claimed to have seen the child, the search team spotted Matunde from a distance. When Matunde saw the approaching search team, he stood up and started running towards the bushes. Although the team members tried everything in their power to pursue the child, they could not succeed in catching him. A report was then given to the chief who could not believe the search team members' account of their pursuit. The villagers were also astonished as they felt it was unimaginable for a barefooted boy to outpace members of the search team in such a rocky terrain.

It was then decided that it would be in the interest of the child to consult a traditional healer to shed light on the circumstance facing the village regarding the child's unexplained behaviour. The traditional healer set up and doctored a special search team which was instructed to go and wait for Matunde to appear at the same place he was spotted by

64

the shepherds. Just before sunset, the boy emerged from the bush and sat on an elevated hill. Although the plan was to "ambush" Matunde, it took the team sometime to apprehend him. The boy was disorientated and could not talk or recognize anyone, including the family members.

Given the mysterious circumstance and lack of explanation(s) from Matunde thereof, the community decided to seek further assistance from a traditional healer. A different healer from a distant village was suggested. The community felt that, amidst the mistrust and hype that had developed within the community during the search, a healer who was not privy to the situation would be impartial in the diagnosis of the enigmatic problem facing the community.

Although the consultation with the traditional healer only lasted a day and Matunde miraculously gained his memory and speech, the healer kept the child for another four days for observation and treatment. Once the treatment was over, a meeting attended by the village elders and the boy's parents was called where the Matunde was given an opportunity to narrate what had happened.

Matunde said: "I was staying at Mr Mudau's orchard where there are other terrifying people such as Ms K, Mr B and Ms R." The names mentioned by the child were of the people whom the community knew as dead and buried, although their death were somewhat regarded as a "mystery" by some community members.

Matunde claimed that Mr Mudau compelled the mysterious people in his orchard to work during the night. These people were starved and only fed once at night. He stated that Mr Mudau told him that he was going to be a shepherd and would soon join the other people in the orchard. The boy further claimed that it was only after seeing the mysterious people at Mr Mudau's orchard that he could neither speak nor comprehend what was going on.

Based on Matunde's account, the elders decided concluded that Mudau possessed zombies, these are the living dead who are resurrected from graves and made to work for the witches under cover of darkness. They claimed that Matunde was in the process of being turned into a zombie. They called for a community meeting where Mr Mudau was a special guest of the chief. The allegations made by the boy were presented to Mr Mudau who did not deny them. Mr Mudau was instantly banished from the village.

While the handling of the case by the chief and the elders was illegal, the process followed and the decision taken was unfair to Mr Mudau; the intervention was however effective in that it prevented violence and subsequent loss of life. As demonstrated by the above case, healers also play a central role in neutralising witches at the level of community. In Venda, a healer who is a member of the traditional council ensures the protection of the whole village during certain seasons. He or she advises the council on which healer to be hired by the community to protect the traditional council as well as the whole village.

In Kom, a healer who is in the council works together with all the jujus and other healers in a *ngvin* society in the whole of Kom to protect all the villages from the attack of witches. They cut the leaves and herbs of some medicinal plants, and mix them with wood ash. The wild aubergine is broken and the medicine is put inside. Certain rituals are then carried out before the medicine is thrown on all village squares, road junctions, bridges, overhanging rivers and streams, entrances into homesteads, doorposts and on farms. Members of *ngvin* society hold a fowl which is passed from one member to the other, uttering their wishes with regard to what the medicine should do to the Muso witches. They do so while spitting (*sifam*) on the fowl. When the ritual is complete, the fowl is sacrificed. This is done by throwing the head of the fowl on any hard object which cuts it off. Any witch who tries to cross this medicine is killed. Upon witches' arrival, the medicine blinds them by covering the village with a mountain or sea, which is invisible to ordinary people. Once blinded, witches get confused and end up walking into natural hills and large trees. It is owing to the protection offered by healers that witches are now known to have resorted to getting into calabashes that float them down streams as they buzz like bees in order to enter villages. Here again, the healers have responded by placing medicine in calabashes and tying them under bridges in an attempt to prevent witches from entering the villages.

In Kom it was observed that, unlike in Venda, traditional authorities were empowered by the law to deal with witchcraft cases. As it will become evident below, these institutions are highly active and enjoy legitimacy on matters of custom and tradition.

Ngwainkuma traditional council in Kom

The council is made up of twenty-eight councillors, and is headed by a president who is simultaneously the village chief. The president works closely with the chairperson, treasurer, secretary and the messenger, who are all voted into their positions by village members. Council members who occupy these four portfolios can represent the council anywhere. The messenger is the one who runs errands for the traditional council, serving summons to both the accuser and accused. He is also the spokesperson of the traditional council as well as the town crier. He informs villagers of the decisions arrived at in the council. Members are generally elected by a show of hands every four years. For voting to take place, villagers assemble at the chief's place, candidates are nominated and are asked to move into a compound, the name of a candidate is mentioned and villagers are asked to vote.

Council members are people with exceptional conduct, men and women of virtue and good character, people who can talk, who are kind, patient and generous. Youths are also part of the council and do play an active role. There is a Kom saying that "if a child washes his or her hands clean, such a child can eat with his or her elders." A well-mannered youth is therefore allowed to participate in decision-making processes even though issues at hand concern adults. The mixed composition of the council is a reflection of the variety of cases dealt with by the council.

All but witchcraft cases are reported to the traditional council by one of the feuding parties. Witchcraft cases are reported to a village juju who before reporting the case to the traditional council makes several consultations with specialists like *ngambe*. If the juju discovers that the sick person has his or her heart, footprints, clothes or hair taken away to be "eaten" by a witch, the juju summons all the

67

villagers and announces that the witch who is already known to the juju alone and is eating the sick man should withdraw his or her witchcraft. This is usually done at a big village assembly in the chief's compound. If the witch does not set his or her victim free, then the name of the witch is made public.

The matter is then reported to the secretary who registers it and prepares a notice, which demands that feuding parties should appear before the council on a particular day. When served with a notice feuding parties should each bring 1225FCFA[21]. Of this amount 25FCFA is for the notice, 200FCFA for buying a fowl for the messenger, and 1000FCFA goes to the traditional council. The council may be convened to look into the matter and invite feuding parties to explain themselves. Council members deliberate on the matter before putting it to a vote. Decisions are taken on the basis of a simple majority. Once a decision is taken, the president may still veto it.

If either of the feuding parties disagrees with the decision of the council, some council members together with selected people closer to both the feuding parties visit a *ngambe* to find out the truth. If a *ngambe* does not find the accused guilty, then the accuser is ordered to pay for defamation of character. If the accused is confirmed guilty, the elders call him or her to order and settle the matter. If the accused repeats the act after the judgment, then he or she is banished from the village. Alternatively, the accused who is confirmed guilty by a *ngambe* may be asked by the elders to pay for his or her witchcraft actions in a number of ways. The accused may be asked to offer fowls or goats, or may be banned from borrowing a match or lighting a fire in someone's kitchen. He or she may be isolated by fellow villagers until such time that they are satisfied that the dangerous activities have ceased.

The punishment for a witch is usually ostracism. Before this takes place, the town crier informs all the villagers to gather at the chief's place. It is here that the decision to ostracise the witch is announced. The ostracized person may no longer associate with other people,

---

[21] 100 FCFA equals R1.

visit other homesteads, appear in the market, at funerals, death celebrations, village gatherings, or participate in communal works. If someone dies in the home of an ostracized witch, villagers only come to bury and leave immediately without staying to console the witch. Anyone found visiting an ostracized witch may be ostracized too. Ostracism is indefinite until the witch repents and pleads to the village that he or she has abandoned his or her witchcraft. This should however be confirmed by healers. Ostracism only applies to the alleged witch and not to his or her family. If the witch is found to be disobedient at this level, then the case is sent to the Kwifoyn in the Kom palace.

The Kwifoyn banishes a witch from Kom

Community containment of witchcraft in Kom is more pronounced and coordinated than in Venda. If a witchcraft case is unresolved by a traditional council at village level in Kom, it is passed to Laikom to be handled by the Kwifoyn, which is the Executive Council of Kom. Kwifoyn is an institution composed of functionaries, selected and trained for the execution of the affairs of the kingdom. It has the authority to carry out decisions or decrees issued by the Foyn or his advisers or court. Nkwi (1976:64) wrote that "the Kwifoyn did not constitute the government as such but it had a pivotal role in government. It provided the Foyn with a police force, emissaries or envoys and economists for the royal household... It was charged with the proper functioning of the Foyn's administrative institutions." The Kwifoyn safeguards and protects the customs, the culture and the tradition of the Kom people.

The Kwifoyn is staffed by male figures called Nchisendo, who are regarded as the eyes, ears and mouths of the Kwifoyn. They are charged with a multiplicity of functions. They apprehend wrongdoers, police the market, inflict punishments imposed by the Foyn and his council, try cases of witchcraft, murder and adultery committed by the Foyn's wives, discipline their fellow members and deal with infringements of their injunctions. Penalties vary from prohibitions of movement, use of disputed land, raffia and kola plantations, and immobilisation of persons for breaches of law (Nkwi, 1976:89).

Any alleged witch who defies a decision of a traditional council is taken to the Kwifoyn for a further trial. If found guilty by the Kwifoyn, the alleged witch is heavily fined; that is, the fine that they were supposed to pay at the village level is doubled. He or she has to pay ten fowls, ten goats, and two jugs of palm-wine to the Kwifoyn. If the alleged witch defies the Kwifoyn's judgment, the Kwifoyn moves to all the three major Kom markets[22]to reach all the *tutangti kom bulamo*[23], the nine Kom hills, and announce the kind of punishment that has been meted out to the alleged witch. This announcement carries detailed information on the harm that the alleged witch has inflicted on the victim, village and Kom as a whole.

The announcement by the Kwifoyn is made on a market day[24]because it is believed that most people will be present, particularly all the clans for whom the information is intended. People rush to the market once they hear that the Kwifoyn is there. When the announcement is to be made, the Nchisendo assemble and stand in a long line. A juju leads the Nchisendo into the market.

The Nchindo who makes the pronouncement carries with him a very long bamboo. He is always half-naked. He wears a loincloth, and is rubbed with medicines that protect him against harm, natural or manmade. His face is rubbed with camwood, which puts him in a

---

[22] A market in Kom is a point of convergence. People come from all the four corners of Kom to buy, sell or entertain themselves with friends in the market. The major markets in Kom are Fundong, Belo and Njinikom markets. These are the markets used by the Kwifoyn in case it has some information to pass over to the Kom people. Since it is in these markets that people from all the tutangti kom bulamo or nine Kom hills or villages can be met, the Kwifoyn uses these markets or convergent points of Kom as a medium for the dissemination or passing over of its messages. The message comes from the Kwifoyn but the announcement of this message is made by a Nchindo. Announcing any message in these markets means announcing it to all the Kom people.

[23] They are Mbengkas, Baiso, Mejang, Baicham, Akeh, Achain, Ajung, Mbessinaku, and Mbueni.

[24] The day in which the Kwifoyn comes to the market is referred to as the ntum-kwifoyn.

70

trance. When the Nchindɔ enters the market, the talking in the market suddenly ceases and the people are obliged to remain silent and listen to the Kwifoyn's message.

Once the message is delivered, it spreads like wild fire over Kom. All those people who were in the market at the time of the Kwifoyn's pronouncement quickly disseminate the news, usually in a spontaneous manner. For instance, if one greets the other and says "how are you?" the other's response is "yesterday in the market the Kwifoyn said..." This is the type of greeting response that is expected from every person in Kom once the Kwifoyn has made an announcement in the market.

Below is an announcement by the Kwifoyn that I witnessed on Tuesday, 29 August 2000 which involved the banishing of an alleged witch. It happened in the village of Mbam, about 5 kilometres away from where I was staying at the time. My two research assistants and I were informed the previous day by the main juju that the Kwifoyn would be banishing an alleged witch the following day. In the following morning we were already in the village where the announcement was to be made by 08h30. At 10h00 we saw villagers heading towards us in the market place. Within a short time, the market was full of people.

Before heading to the market, the Kwifoyn first planted the *alang a Kwifoyn* at the home of the alleged witch as a symbol of banishing the *avung* from Mbam. The Kwifoyn then proceeded to Mbam market to announce the banishment which was made by a Nchindo.

Case 8: The banishment of *avung* Peter Ngàm from Mbam in Kom

PARA ONE:

Mbam! O - o Mbam! O - ɔ - o Mba-am! I have always been pinning my sticks[25] *into the gateways of villages. They are two sticks, m-m-m, my eyes in every*

---

[25] These "two sticks" are symbolically the Nchisendo (Foyn's Messengers or Policemen) and the Mugwo Chu' who is the juju that detects and unmasks anyone practicing witchcraft. The juju also protects homesteads and villages against witches.

village! They watch any good or bad thing that enters or leaves the village, and employ appropriate sanctions when necessary. Mbam, why do you practise bad Muso (witchcraft) to the extent that the good things that used to be in Mbam are no longer present? There are many gossips in Mbam; the child's "Fubom"[26] or calabash for preserving his drinking water is gone. The child's camwood[27] is also gone. The bad Muso has been causing stillbirths in Mbam. Mugwo Chu' is suffering because when this juju washes women with medicine in a bid to make them fertile or reproductive, these bad witches always come to destroy these babies, causing stillbirths. Let these witches be warned of my supernatural strength: they will climb a tree thinking they are ahead of me and they will meet me coming downward.

PARA TWO:

Now I tell you the issue that brings me to Mbam: It is the issue of Peter Ngàm's witchcraft. Peter Ngàm has planted bad medicine in Mbam. Peter Ngàm, what is it that you have against Mbam? You are a Kom child. You grew up in one quarter, and were relocated. On arriving in another quarter, you were again relocated... You came and settled in Mbam and Mbam embraced you. If I am standing and you, Peter Ngàm, are inside the compound, you should only remain inside the compound. Your wives should only go to the farm, passing only through the bush road without reaching where I am standing. No one should pass there.

PARA THREE:

When I first summoned Ngàm to come and have his case heard, he first refused and went to the White Man's Administration. I, Kwifoyn at dawn and Kwifoyn even here present, have lost my reputation. This is because of those witches like Ngàm who, instead of resolving their disputes through the traditional councils, take the issue to the White Man's Administration. These witches that take me to the White Man's Administration must be ostracized. They should not be visited even during moments of grief or joy. They should not light fire or borrow a match. They should not attend

---

[26] This is a small long-necked round bottom calabash stuck with the peace plant "Nke," as it is called here containing a baby's drinking water.

[27] Camwood symbolises fecundity. It is rubbed on the head and body of brides, successors, Foyns, enthronements, and young women who are giving birth for the first time.

72

major village gatherings like festivals and death celebrations. My pronouncements are not limited to Mbam alone, but to all the Tutangti kom bulamo (nine hills of Kom).

PARA FOUR:
Thanks to the fumbuen[28] for allowing me to come to Mbam. Fumbuen should not sleep. But when you go somewhere to do things, you should not rush over them. If you hear any gossip, you should sit down and examine it carefully, come back to the village elders so that they should carefully tell you the said matter. Again I say to all of you, never take issues of custom and tradition to the White Man's Administration. This does not mean that when a villager butchers another, when someone cuts down someone's coffee, destroys someone's crops or ridges, he or she should not be taken to the White Man's Administration. Customary issues like witchcraft, planting of medicine, and removal of its injunction stick, should be taken to institutions with traditional jurisdiction. To any witch I say: if you are brought to me you should confess and make your will because medicine will be given to you to eat. This poisonous medicine will kill you if you are guilty of the witchcraft act. If not responsible for the act, you will simply vomit the medicine.

PARA FIVE:
Mugwò Chu' and fumbuen, you should hold up the peace in Mbam. Bò Mbam, you should not sleep, you should remain alert and speak out about whatever bad thing you see. You should not be influenced to tell lies because if you do, I will know. I say this because I know that my Nchìsendo are suffering. For they have fallen prey to this incident. I'm now telling Mbam that I have removed all the said Nchìsendo, and have only left those who are moving foot-to-foot with Mbam. And you medicine men should give my people only good medicine to cure and not those that kill. You should work under the authority of Bò Mbam.

The above announcement by the Kwifoyn provides insight into the life of villagers in a witchcraft-ridden society. Firstly in Para One,

---

[28] The *fumbuen* also gets involved in the punishment of a witch. The women sing their dirges on a witch when caught, and would trample a witch to force a confession. They at times collect dirt from the village and dump it at the witch's place. This is also the main institution that gets involved in the destruction of the witch's property.

the Kwifoyn expresses its awareness of the proliferation of witchcraft and the harm it is inflicting on villagers. The Kwifoyn tells villagers that it is conscious of their concerns about the increasing uncontrollable actions of witches. It reminds villagers of its omnipotent supernatural strength to detect the occult force in all villages of Kom. It assures villagers that the Nchisendo and the Kom juju are working day and night to bring this witchcraft under control. This introduction is crucial in that it allays the fear that villagers have about witchcraft and takes away their sense of helplessness in the face of this occult force.

Secondly, the announcement demonstrates that in societies where traditional authorities are entrusted with powers to preside over witchcraft matters, their intervention is effective in saving life as well as in averting uncontrollable violence. Peter Ngàm has a reputation as a witch who 'eats' his victims in every village he settles in. In response to his witchcraft, traditional councils offered him protection by moving him from one village to the other. The Kwifoyn makes this revelation in paragraph 2 when it addresses Peter Ngàm that *you are a Kom child. You grew up in one quarter, and were relocated. On arriving in another quarter, you were again relocated... You came and settled in Mbam. Mbam embraced you.*

In my interaction with villagers, it was revealed that Peter Ngàm used to live in Baingo village at Belo Subdivision where he was banished for 'eating' people with his witchcraft. He moved to Ngwainkuma village in Fundong Subdivision where he was again banished for trying to 'eat' fellow villagers. He went and pleaded with the late chief of Mbam village who gave him a piece of land to build on. In Mbam, Peter Ngàm is accused of having 'eaten' and even threatening a number of people. In its response, the Kwifoyn decides to banish Mbam from Kom. While this form of punishment is considered extreme, it prevents violence and loss of life. Such a careful and responsible management of witchcraft disputes is absent in segmentary societies or in Venda where traditional authorities are incapacitated by law and where everyone is involved in deciding the fate of an alleged witch.

While the Kwifoyn's role in witchcraft disputes saves lives, the all-encompassing nature of its punishment is a source of concern to villagers. In banishing Peter Ngàm, the Kwifoyn further states that *your wives should only go to the farm, passing only through the bush road without reaching where I am standing. No one should pass there.* By this utterance, the Kwifoyn not only banishes Peter Ngàm, but it also ostracises his wives. Punishments that are also meted out to family members of the wrongdoer, such as this one, are often not well received by villagers. There is often a feeling that an alleged witch should be banished alone and that his or her family should be left to continue leading a normal life. The family of the alleged witch should be allowed to continue using the homestead, or follow the banished witch if they so choose.

Thirdly, the announcement shows that effective as the institution of traditional authority may be in preventing witchcraft violence and murders, its execution of duty and decisions do not enjoy overall legitimacy. In paragraph 3, the Kwifoyn complains to the Kom people that *I, Kwifoyn at dawn and Kwifoyn even here present, have lost my reputation. This is because of those witches like Ngàm who, instead of resolving their disputes through the traditional councils, take the issue to the White Man's Administration.* These remarks show that, revered as the Kwifoyn may be on most matters of tradition, not all villagers agree with the way it deals with witchcraft cases. When Peter Ngàm was first invited to the traditional council to account for his witchcraft, he turned down the invitation. When invited for the second time, he again rejected the invitation. He only turned up after the third invitation. He was asked to pay a fine for not obeying the calls of the traditional council. He was also asked to contribute money so that a delegation could go to consult a *ngambe* from a distant place. He refused and instead took the matter to the Divisional Officer of Fundong. The officer invited the *fumbuen*, village elders and traditional councillors to his office to answer the case lodged by Peter Ngàm against Mbam village. After some discussion, the officer stated that the matter fell under the jurisdiction of the traditional council in the village. Peter Ngàm persistently refused to submit himself to the traditional council until his case was handed over to the Kwifoyn.

Peter Ngàm is by no means the only villager who contests the Kwifoyn's authority. Some villagers believe that the Kwifoyn is undemocratic in its actions and that its decisions are often shrouded in controversy. They feel coerced to subscribe to the Kwifoyn's authority even when they do not believe that the institution is resolving witchcraft cases in an agreeable manner. An element of force is evident in paragraph 3 when the Kwifoyn orders that *these witches that take me to the White Man's Administration must be ostracized. They should not be visited even during moments of grief or joy. They should not light fire or borrow a match. They should not attend major village gatherings like festivals and death celebrations.*

Fourthly, the Kwifoyn makes a reference to a poison that is forced on witches when taken to Laikom. The poison is given to those witches that are deemed not to own up to their witchcraft. The Kwifoyn warns witches, in paragraph 4, that *if you are brought to me you should confess and make your will because medicine will be given to you to eat. This poisonous medicine will kill you if you are guilty of the witchcraft act. If not responsible for the act, you will simply vomit the medicine.* Traditional authorities across Kom deny that witches have been forced to swallow poisonous medicine to force confessions from them. Some villagers however claim that it is the fear of dying from such poisonous medicine which often results in some innocent accused giving false confessions. Traditional councils however admit that, before the passing of the Penal Code of 1967, witches used to be subjected to illegal forms of punishment such as torture, small sticks being pierced into the tips of witches' fingernails, witches being tied up from the roof while pepper is burnt in the fire so that they can be choked with the resultant smoke, and witches were killed by pushing them down a hill. They claim that since the recognition of the belief in witchcraft and tacit recognition given to traditional authorities to deal with matters of custom and tradition, it is no longer possible for a witch to be killed with impunity by either villagers or traditional councils. Traditional authorities know they are now accountable to government authorities, and are responsible for any witchcraft killing that occurs within their area of jurisdiction.

Fifthly, the Kwifoyn encourages the chief of Mbam to remain 'alert' and to continue to 'speak out' and 'not be influenced to tell lies'. This call reveals that, in its efforts to resolve witchcraft disputes, the institution of traditional leadership is not free of corrupt practices that may amount to unfairness and injustice. Throughout Kom, rumour was rife that certain notorious witches were immune to the punishment of the Kwifoyn owing to their close relationship with some organs of the traditional authority.

In their comparative study of witchcraft in two regions of Cameroon, Geschiere and Nyamnjoh (1998:87) showed that "even in the highly structured societies of the Grassfields, with their elaborate institutional constructions for legitimising hierarchy, such traditional interventions [on witchcraft matters] are always highly precarious. The foyn of Bum was [in his intervention over witchcraft matters] more or less openly accused of letting the main culprit get away in exchange for certain presents." Such is a demonstration that the institution of traditional authority is not free of corrupt practices.

The Kwifoyn is also not immune to divisions and malpractices amongst its members. This emerges from last paragraph when the Kwifoyn warns the chief of Mbam not to lie and states that *as I say this I know that my nchisendo are suffering. For they have fallen prey to this incident. I'm now telling Mbam that I have removed all the said nchisendo, and have only left those who are moving foot-to-foot with Mbam.* This reference to the dismissal of two nchisendo – Nge' Nazhia and John Akoni – during the announcement is an indication of the controversial nature of some members of the Kwifoyn, which tends to raise questions over the legitimacy of some of its decisions.

Lastly and generally, throughout the announcement, the Kwifoyn makes reference to various actors and the roles they play in the containment of witchcraft. The actors are, amongst others, the Kom juju, the chief of Mbam, medicine men, the Nchisendo, the *fumbuen* and the village elders. For example, in paragraph 4, the Kwifoyn provides a differentiation of roles when it says that the *fumbuen* should not 'rush over' punishing alleged witches and advises *if you hear any gossip, you should sit down and examine it carefully, come back to the village elders so that they should carefully tell you the said matter.* A warning is given

77

here that witchcraft accusations are not always sincere and without motive, and that rushing to punish alleged witches may result in the victimisation of innocent people. Hence the Kwifoyn advises the *fumbuen* that in discharging its responsibilities, it should constantly consult the village elders. This call is similar to those that the Kwifoyn make to other actors, throughout its announcement, on the need for them to efficiently execute their respective duties. This awareness about different actors and their roles in the management of witchcraft cases in Kom is a feature that has eroded in Venda. In my meetings with the youths in Kom, I was struck by their acceptance that witchcraft was the exclusive domain of elderly people, and that traditional councils were the best forums for the mediation of disputes arising from this occult force. In Venda however, youths believed that it was upon them to free their communities of witches.

Conclusion

It has been demonstrated in this chapter that the containment of witchcraft can be found at both family and community levels, and that the institutions of traditional healing and traditional leadership are central in such containment. Both institutions work more as points of crystallization. They prevent confrontation between the accuser and the accused, while absorbing the stress, fear and anger that both feuding parties may experience as a result of a witchcraft incident. Generally, they also provide a sense of security to community members from the perceived daily threat of witchcraft.

In Venda however, traditional healers play an ambiguous role in witchcraft matters. On the one hand, traditional healers provide villagers with needed fortification against witchcraft attack. The protection ensures that there is often no confrontation between the witch and the bewitched. On the other hand, traditional healers play a role of witch identification in some witchcraft cases. This role is controversial in that it generates accusations and often results in witchcraft violence and murders. In accordance with the law, traditional authorities refuse to deal with witchcraft cases, thereby

78

creating a vacuum that may be exploited by vigilantes as it shall be demonstrated in the next chapter.

Contrary to their counterparts in Venda, traditional authorities in Kom are vibrant, and play a crucial role in resolving witchcraft disputes. Traditional authorities see themselves as an auxiliary to the state. They are accountable to the state on matters of tradition and custom. They therefore ensure that they maintain control over traditional healers and community members on issues relating to witchcraft. This explains why there is lower witchcraft violence in Kom than in Venda despite the prevalence of witchcraft beliefs and practices in both societies.

Chapter Four

Explaining Witchcraft Violence in Venda, Limpopo Province

Introduction

Levels and types of belief in witches vary in time within African societies. At some points in time people believe that witches are rife and more aggressive within their communities; while at other points they believe that while witches exist, they show signs of domesticity and are confinable. The witchcraft violence that has ravaged the area of Venda since the 1980s manifests such variation in the beliefs as held by people in witchcraft-ridden communities.

The twentieth century, and particularly its last two decades, has witnessed an effort in anthropology to situate African witchcraft within social 'strain-gauge' and modernity theories. This was done as if African witchcraft it was homogeneous and coherent, and notwithstanding its variations in different African localities. African witchcraft has therefore increasingly become a phenomenon that is understood within the context of recent socio-economic changes that have engulfed the globe. Similarly, the witchcraft violence that left large parts of the Limpopo Province divided and counting the loss of their inhabitants has been explained in terms of these theories. The violence was said to have been instigated by unemployed and disillusioned youth against the elderly or the jealous poor against the relatively rich whom they blamed for their sufferings. It was said to reflect a "widespread anxiety about the production and reproduction of wealth, an anxiety that translated into bitter generational opposition. ... It should be noted, urban "comrades" demonised the parental generation as passive "sell-outs" to colonial oppression ... Precisely this sense of illegitimate production and reproduction pervades youthful discourses of witchcraft in much of South Africa. Many young blacks blame their incapacity to ensure a future for

81

themselves on an aged elite that controls the means of generating wealth without working" (Comaroff and Comaroff 1997:19). That is, the impoverished youth perpetuated this violence against the relatively better off elderly people.

Such a dichotomous explanation of witchcraft violence in areas of the Limpopo Province was also echoed in the media. In *Ke Bona Boloi*, a drama on witchcraft violence in the Limpopo Province that was broadcast on SABC TV (South Africa's public broadcasting television station) in 1999, the disgruntled, unemployed, partisan youth were portrayed as the perpetrators of the violence against the elderly, especially old women. Meanwhile, the diviners were portrayed as quacks and charlatans who were central to the witchcraft violence. Those accused of witchcraft were portrayed as victims of loose gossip, jealousy or as members of the community who were vulnerable and weak. They were victims of social insanity arising from irrational community members that were struggling to make sense of their sufferings as a result of socio-economic changes.

However, reducing the witchcraft violence that ravaged the Limpopo Province into conventional and commonplace explanations is too simple. Without analysing such violence within the social context that it takes place, such efforts actually yields little understanding. What happened in Venda and other areas was a witchcraft struggle which centred around a collective determination to rid communities of witches. In Venda, participation in this witchcraft struggle was not shaped by party-political identification, poverty, wealth, gender or age, but was influenced by fear – the fear of becoming the next victim of witchcraft and the fear of being labelled a witch. This fear and the awareness of fear cut across members of society - political leaders, traditional leaders, traditional healers, church leaders, academics, and members of the police service - who were caught up in witchcraft struggle.

It was this witchcraft struggle that divided members of various communities into heroes and villains. In this respect, it resembled the struggle for liberation, which divided the black community in South Africa into those who supported the liberation movements and those who accepted the oppressive system. As in the liberation struggle, neutrality in the witchcraft struggle was unacceptable and was often interpreted as covert support for witches and the State which was deemed as apathetic to the concerns of the majority of its citizens. The heroes were those that saw themselves as committed to freeing the community from the supernatural evil - liberating people from the attacks of witches. They called themselves comrades – a popular name within political circles during the struggle for liberation. The villains were those labelled as witches, their relatives, and everyone who was viewed as sympathizing with them.

This chapter critically examines the work of authors who view witchcraft attributions and accusations as both a gauge for strained social relations and as a reflection of people's frustrations that are the consequence of current socio-economic changes. Although strained social relations and modernity are important, they cannot be viewed as the only, or even the most important explanations for witchcraft violence that took place in Limpopo Province. Strained social relations and modernity, as explanations for witchcraft violence, should be viewed within the context of both the politics of the South African state during apartheid and the ontology of witchcraft in the communities concerned.

An understanding of witchcraft violence in Venda can be better reached when considering the controversial role played by the Apartheid State in this occult domain. The state, by outlawing traditional healers and the role of traditional councils in witchcraft-related matters and by placing witchcraft-related cases under the jurisdiction of modern courts, incapacitated those institutions whose purpose it was to deal with unrest resulting from witchcraft. Furthermore, the knowledge and experience that the Vhavenda have about witchcraft inform their reactions to witchcraft incidents, thereby leading to variations and unpredictability in witchcraft accusations. This point is elaborated on in this chapter by reflecting on accusations relating to spirit-induced witchcraft.

The aim is therefore to show that people's understanding of various forms of witchcraft leads to variation in their reactions to witchcraft incidents, and that these responses shape the nature of witchcraft accusations. While some accusations may be a climax of recurring conflict, others may, however, occur in an environment characterised by amicable social relations. Therefore, rather than being a mechanism for the expression and resolution of social tensions and conflicts, witchcraft may be a threat to good social relations. The chapter also shows that witchcraft-ridden communities have institutions that deal with witchcraft problems, and that witchcraft policies of modern states impact on the working of these institutions in various ways. A look at this relationship may contribute towards an understanding of witchcraft violence in Venda, and other areas of the Limpopo Province. What follows is an excursive description of the environment in which witchcraft accusations and violence take place. This is done by considering a certain form of witchcraft belief amongst the Vhavenda, and its manifestation in the form of two cases.

The fury of a rejected witchcraft of inheritance

As evident in chapter two, the Vhavenda believe that one can either inherit or buy witchcraft. This chapter, however, concerns itself with inherited witchcraft. As discussed in chapter 2, this type of witchcraft involves blood-thirsty spirits that are either inherited or passed over to a victim in the form of a spell through ritual incantation.

When contracted as a spell and rejected by their supposed inheritor, the spirits usually wreak harm on their supposed inheritor. The spirits can be cast as a spell only by a relative of the supposed inheritor, and usually during marriage time. A relative may send these spirits out of jealousy or discontent over the way a marriage has been arranged. The relative can be of either gender and from either side of the supposed inheritor's lineage. The best-known reason for this type of witchcraft is to ensure that the supposed inheritor never has a happy and lasting marriage.

When rejected by their supposed inheritor, the spirits unleash their fury by tormenting their supposed inheritor, at times with fatal consequences. They render the supposed male inheritor barren or gradually consume his soul until death. The supposed male inheritor will, owing to his barrenness, lose one wife after the other. They reveal themselves to the supposed female inheritor during pregnancy. She will not be able to deliver a baby unless she submits a soul as an offering,

84

preferably a relative of her husband. In the absence of a relative, an associate (concubine or friend) of the supposed female inheritor would suffice. In such cases, the old soul is sacrificed for the coming of a new one. The supposed inheritors may, however, be cleansed and saved by traditional healers through the performance of certain rituals and the application of medicines.

Described below are two spirit-induced witchcraft cases that were recounted to me during fieldwork. These cases involve two women who lost their relatives each time they were pregnant and about to deliver. As it will become evident, the knowledge that these women's in-laws (their accusers) possess about this form of witchcraft shapes their reactions to witchcraft incidents each time they occur, thereby making witchcraft accusations vary and unpredictable.

Case 9: Mashau: Spirit-induced witchcraft as a curse in Venda

I was recounted one case of spirit-induced witchcraft in the village of Khalavha which involved Mashau, a 43-year-old woman who was married to Makungo. The couple had two daughters, aged 20 and 13. Makungo worked in the city, and returned home twice a year, in June and December. Mashau was married into a family of four, consisting of Makungo, Masindi (her husband's mother), Mashango and Mavhele (her husband's brother and sister respectively). In 1978, a year after the marriage, Mashau went temporarily insane for some months, often stripping her clothes off and running amok. Makungo returned home to help his wife recover from this sudden illness. After five months, Mashau was recovered and fell pregnant in mid-1979. Some months later, Masindi died from strangulation, and two weeks later Mashau gave birth to a girl who was named Musiiwa.

Mashau became pregnant again in 1986, and gave birth to her second daughter, Thili, in 1987. Three weeks before Thili was born, Mashango died from strangulation. After the burial, Makungo asked Nyamunzhedzi (Masindi's elder sister) to come and stay with Mashau and Mavhele. The old woman refused, blaming Mashau's witchcraft for causing the deaths of Masindi and Mashango. She demanded that

Mashau's problem should be attended to before she could move in. Makungo then left for the city, leaving behind his wife and sister.

Things took a turn for the worse in 1999 when Makungo unexpectedly returned home in October. Three weeks after his return, Makungo was terminally ill. On realising that her husband's health was deteriorating, Mashau informed Nyamunzhedzi that her husband had not been able to excrete for five days, the centre of his head had become soft while his scrotum kept on bulging. These are the symptoms associated with *u wela* (an illness which is suffered by a man who went to bed with a woman who had induced an abortion). The old lady feared for Makungo's life since she thought it would be difficult to find a cure. The traditional treatment for this illness involves the woman with whom the inflicted man went to bed. In Makungo's case Nyamunzhedzi thought the culprit would not be readily available since she could be in the city. To the surprise of Nyamunzhedzi, Mashau confessed she went to bed with her husband some weeks after she had induced an abortion. The conception of the aborted pregnancy took place during June when Makungo was home. When she found out she was pregnant, Mashau could not bear the thought of having another member in the family dying, probably her husband's only remaining sibling, Mavhele. It was for this reason that Mashau decided to get rid of the unborn baby so as to save the soul that was already in the family. She had intended to get cleansed before Makungo returned from the city in December. Things went beyond her control with Makungo's unexpected return.

Upon hearing the confession from Mashau, Nyamunzhedzi took Makungo for treatment to Khakhu, a renowned traditional healer in the village. Makungo was completely cured after three weeks. He then asked Khakhu to look into the real cause of the problem his wife was facing. Khakhu found that Mashau had been given a spell at marriage by her uncle, who was worried that he was not given a share of Mashau's *thakha* (bridewealth) despite the fact that he had spent a great deal raising her. The uncle cursed Mashau with the intention of getting her returned by her in-laws once they discovered she was a witch. Khakhu advised the couple to stop bearing children while a solution to the problem was being sought. She also recommended that Mavhele be relocated since she was likely to become the next victim should Mashau

86

become pregnant again. Mavhele then left the family to stay with relatives in a distant village.

Case 3, Donga: Spirit-induced witchcraft as inheritance in Venda

In the same village lived Manyaru; a well-known rich man, aged 55. He was one of the four children (two sons and two daughters) born of a single parent. Manyaru had a big modern house in the village. In it lived his mother, his brother, and his younger sister and her two children. He also had a house in the city, and was staying there for the past twenty years. Manyaru was married to a Motswana woman with whom he lived in the city of Johannesburg. Manyaru's long stay in the city was a concern among his family members in the village. His marriage to a woman of another ethnic group became a constant pain. His relatives feared that Manyaru would follow most men in the countryside who went to work in the city and married a woman of another ethnic group and never returned home. Their fear was exacerbated not only by the fact that Manyaru was a breadwinner, but also that he had been providing for the family of his elder sister (a divorcee with four children - one son and three daughters). As a result, these family members in the rural area decided that Manyaru should marry a second wife, who was to remain in the village. The plan was for this woman to bear children that would connect Manyaru to the village.

Donga (Manyaru's second and village wife) was married in 1986, and later had three children. A member of the Manyaru family had passed away each time Donga was to bear a child. Donga became pregnant for the fourth time in the early part of 1999. Things turned sour when Tshilidzi and Mahada[29] threatened Donga with a hatchet.

---

[29] Tshilidzi and Mahada are Manyaru's nephew and niece respectively. They are the children of Manyaru's elder sister. Tshilidzi is a taxi driver (the taxi was bought for him by Manyaru). Mahada is a student at the University of Venda. She was back home on winter recess. The University of Venda is one of the two universities in the Limpopo Province. It is about 25 kilometres from Khalavha village.

Donga ran to *musanda* (palace) for protection.[30] Upon hearing Donga's story, the chief called for an emergency meeting of the Executive Council of his *khoro*. Donga's in-law family was summoned to attend the meeting. It was heard that Tshilidzi and Mahada wanted to kill Donga because they feared for their lives: neither of them wanted to become the next victim of Donga's fourth pregnancy. It was revealed that three members of the family (Manyaru's younger brother and Tshilidzi's two sisters) had each passed away during the past three pregnancies. This was a fact that was not disputed by Donga. However, she indicated that she did not understand why this was happening.

The Executive Council members probed into Donga's background. Donga disclosed that her mother was a divorcee who was chased away by her in-laws for the same reason: she gave birth to four children, and each time she did so a family member passed away which was blamed on her. After suspecting that there was witchcraft involved, members of the council summoned Manyaru from the city. Together with his relatives, Manyaru was advised to strongly condemn Tshilidzi's behaviour and to either return Donga to her mother's family or accept Donga back into the family. After some deliberations, the family members advised Manyaru to retain Donga as his wife. Donga, however, decided to stay with her mother until she delivered. She had a miscarriage four months later. She later returned to her in-laws.

When I interviewed several persons involved in this case, certain issues came to the surface: Manyaru's mother indicated that she did not suspect Donga (not even her family) of witchcraft; or, otherwise, she would never have got her married to her son. She expressed her admiration for her daughter-in-law. According to her, Donga had her first born in 1988 and this time Manyaru's brother passed away. The divination they consulted after the burial of her son pointed out that the culprit was in the family. The elderly people, however, decided to let the matter rest. In 1992, Donga had her second born. This time Manyaru's elder sister's daughter passed away by strangulation. In 1997, Donga had

---

[30] This was an aberration of tradition. Normally the procedure requires that any person with a problem report it to *Vhakoma* who would take it to the chief. However, the chief did not feel disrespected on this matter given the emergency of the situation.

her third born and another of Manyaru's elder sister's daughters died of strangulation. These were both Tshilidzi's sisters. The divination set the Manyaru family consulted warned that the tragedy was to repeat unless the elders worked on the problem. When Donga fell pregnant in 1999, the elders were trying to find a solution to Donga's witchcraft problem, and they were doing so sensitively without leaking it to the children. Manyaru's mother said that since the incident the family was again living peacefully like before. She added that the family was working on the problem, and was optimistic that it would be solved soon.

Donga said she was again staying happily with the rest of the family members. She thanked the traditional council for coming to her rescue. She strongly believed that she could have been killed. She started spelling out to me the names of fellow villagers whose lives were lost in witchcraft violence in the past years. She indicated that she had always had a good relationship with Tshilidzi. She believed he acted out of fear. She however did not believe Tshilidzi would die since she had never intended to kill anyone. Meanwhile she did not dismiss that someone would die while she was delivering given the previous experiences. Donga went further to say that the information about her pregnancy was passed over to Tshilidzi and Mahada by a source from outside the family. It was a student nurse – who attended to her at a local clinic – that told Mahada since they were friends from the university. Mahada then passed the information to her brother Tshilidzi.

Mutevhe, a member of the Executive Council and secretary of the traditional council, indicated that they have been handling witchcraft-related cases since 1994. They have been doing this based on the villagers' demands and despite the fact that the law still did not permit such. He indicated that members of the Executive Council took extra care in dealing with cases related to witchcraft, and that they decided to refer to them as "family squabbles" and not "witchcraft cases" any longer, so they could solve them without risk of being prosecuted.

Implications for anthropological theories

The unfolding of events in these cases has implications for anthropological theories and warrant attention. Contrary to

89

anthropological theory that views witchcraft as mechanisms for the expression and resolution of social tensions and conflicts (Seymour-Smith, 1986:289), it can be determined from these cases that witchcraft may at times become a threat to amicable social relations. Mashau and Donga, the two accused women in these cases, have had good relations with their in-laws. In Donga's case, the amicable relations between Donga and her in-laws that seem to have been firmly cemented by the arrangement entered into at marriage, turned sour by the regrettable accusation of witchcraft within the Manyaru family. Indeed, witchcraft becomes the force that threatens to tear apart the previously intact social setting. The arrival of this occult force is regrettable to both the accuser(s) and the accused. Not only is the togetherness with which both the accuser(s) and the accused fight such force a reflection of the good social relations that existed between them, but it also reveals the accusers' understanding of this type of witchcraft, a medium through which the angry spirits wreak harm on people. The Manyaru elders are aware that Donga is a supposed inheritor of witchcraft whose refusal to cooperate with the spirits renders her a victim.

In the case of Mashau, the actors involved in both stages, the consultation of a healer and the arrangement that involves the relocation of Mashau's husband's sister, are the very people that accuse Mashau of witchcraft. Contrary to the social 'strain-gauge' theory that presumes acrimonious relations prior to the levelling of witchcraft accusations, here there is no sign of poor relations between the accuser and the accused: the two antagonists even help one another throughout the crisis. This act indicates the accusers' knowledge and experience of this form of witchcraft, notwithstanding the loss of two family members and the accusations that follow, made it impossible for their relationship with Mashau to become acrimonious. The arrangement to relocate Mavhele reflects the desire on the part of the husband's relatives to retain Mashau as their daughter in-law. By relocating the husband's sister, the elderly people ensure that Mashau stays on as a wife, thus avoiding putting Makungo in a quandary involving his sister and his wife.

If the social tension explanation was valid, and the relationship between Mashau and her in-laws had not been good prior to the

90

accusations, then one would expect the elders to distance themselves from any process aimed at finding a solution to the problem. The elders would do so with the hope that the couple may eventually find it impossible to live together. When social relations have been acrimonious, the elders hardly consider the relocation of the likely victim a possibility, thus leaving the husband with no option but to separate with his wife. However, the accusations here reflect an attempt by the elders to inform Mashau that there is a witchcraft problem, and that she should allow them to help her solve it. Their reaction is informed by their understanding of this type of witchcraft: to them Mashau is as much a victim of her uncle's witchcraft as the two deceased family members.

These two cases typify the variations in witchcraft accusations. While poor relations between the two parties may precede certain accusations, thus making it possible to be able to predict the identity of both the accuser and the accused, in these cases the accusations are characterised by amicable social relations between the two parties. This is an environment that makes witchcraft accusations unpredictable. It would be prudent to recall Niehaus' (1997) caution, in his study of a village situated in the South African Lowveld, that the tendency to view witchcraft accusations as a text for strained social relations can be very misleading. His analysis of several witchcraft accusation cases indicates that, "social and structural tensions by themselves are less accurate predictors of witchcraft attributions and accusations than the literature may lead us to believe," (ibid:252).

Indeed, the way in which the in-laws support their daughters-in-law in chasing out this occult force in these two cases illustrates the harmony that characterised their relationship before these accusations. Both families detected the act of witchcraft immediately after their first or second family member(s) had died. However, they decide to deal with the problem within the families rather than exposing their daughters-in-law to the public during what looked-like an organised campaign to rid the countryside of witches. As in cases that involve other forms of witchcraft, the decision by the accusers to contain the witchcraft privately become a seminal determinant in the survival of the accused. In a witchcraft situation, such as this, that occurs within the family, normally it is the family members that alert other community members of the identity of the witch in the family. The pre-existence of tense relations would have meant that both these families would have used the witchcraft crisis as excuses to get rid of their daughters-in-law.

What then, are the implications of these cases for the "modernity of witchcraft" argument? The modernity explanation argues that witchcraft violence in the Limpopo Province has been perpetrated by frustrated unemployed youth who blame the elderly for their misery. As Comaroff and Comaroff (1997:15-6) explain, ..." for the rural youth mass action may have delivered the vote. But it brought them no nearer to the wealth and empowerment that the overthrow of apartheid was supposed to yield. Quite the reverse. Trade sanctions had dramatically increased unemployment ... Multinational capital is capricious: once apartheid has ended, it found cheaper, more tractable labour and less violence elsewhere. But overall, work is harder to come by and poverty is still dire." As in most cases, the participation of Tshilidzi's sister in the violence does not fare well with this explanation. Mahada is neither frustrated nor roaming the streets in search of employment. She is still a student who regards herself as a future breadwinner. Still, with no exhibition of socio-economic stress, she accompanies Tshilidzi to the killing of Donga. Mahada's case is a typical reflection of youth involvement in witchcraft violence in the Limpopo Province. Most of the youths arrested for perpetrating the violence were the most promising of their communities, school children who saw themselves as future professionals. They were hopeful and positive about the future as opposed to being frustrated and looking for a scapegoat. However, their experience of witchcraft and their fear of becoming a victim of witchcraft drove them to kill alleged witches.

The youth-elderly dichotomy that has become a characteristic of the witchcraft violence – both in the literature and in the media – that has ravaged Venda and other areas of the Limpopo Province is a misrepresentation of what exactly took place. Party-political identification, gender, age, or class fall short of providing adequate explanation for the witchcraft violence that took place in communities in the Limpopo Province. Participation in the witchcraft violence was influenced by fear – the fear of becoming the next victim of witchcraft,

92

and the fear of being labelled a witch. The fear thus unites the community (both the youth and elderly) in an eternal struggle to guard against and warn of any bad use of this mystical power. Once the whistle is blown, a witch is identified and removed. The community remains united regardless of any method used to free the community of witches.

The very youth that are portrayed, both in the media and books, as perpetrators of violence are seen as heroes in these communities, while the real victims of witchcraft violence are seen as villains. The youths are considered saviours. They have delivered their communities from witchcraft which was strangulating fellow villagers at a time when there was no institution to help. In his legal study of witchcraft in East Africa, Mutungi (1977:59) observes, "the killing of a witch is not only approved but... is also a praiseworthy service in the eyes on many communities. For many people believe that the law [suppressing witchcraft] is in collusion with the witches." The following case may help illustrate the collective participation of community members in witchcraft violence:

Case 4: Mandiwana, the haunted village in Venda in 1990

The first half of 1990 saw residents of Mandiwana village engulfed with panic. A couple of girls between the ages of 15 and 22 years died of strangulation in a space of six months. The girls were secondary school pupils and were found hanging in their school uniforms. Every girl began to wonder if she was to die next while other village members began to fear for their lives. In a general meeting of a traditional council, a warning was made to all the witches who could be behind the spate of deaths to stop their evil acts.

There was a rumour that Mutshekwa, an old woman, was responsible for the deaths of the girls. Some parents started advising their children not to use the pathway near Mutshekwa's homestead. It was said that Mutshekwa was using her medicines to target girls that walked past her gate. She would selectively pick up the soil with the footprint of her victims. It was further stated that on 25 September of the same year, Mutshekwa went to the home of Khangwelo, a 16-year-old girl, to propose marriage for her grandson. Khangwelo's mother refused and indicated that her daughter was still young, and that when the time comes she would encourage her to select her own husband. This remark infuriated Mutshekwa and she uttered remarks to the effect that Khangwelo would never get married. In the morning of 01 October, Khangwelo was found hanging on a tree in her school uniform just outside her mother's house.

Two days later, elderly people were nominated to go and visit a healer in a distant place and to find out what had "eaten" the young girl. The healer attributed the death to old Mutshekwa. On the night of 06 October, Mutshekwa was pulled out of a night vigil by a group of men. They stabbed her and dragged her body to a nearby river where they doused it with petrol and set it alight. The men involved were arrested afterwards, and their ages ranged from 15 to 38 years. Six were convicted. Meanwhile, the village experienced an abrupt end to the spate of deaths from strangulation.

The above case reveals a procedure that is usually followed at the death of a family member in Venda. This procedure is central to the investigation of circumstances surrounding the death of a village member, and is usually followed with secrecy, respect and delicacy. Following the death of a family member, elderly relatives usually visit a healer. They visit a healer in a distant place because they reason that such a healer will not falsely accuse a person in their community. The elderly relatives return and call a family gathering where they reveal the verdict of the healer to fellow family members. As it can also be observed from the above case, consulting a healer still remains in most places the exclusive arena of the elderly people. This was notwithstanding the fact that it was largely youths that were subsequently involved in the killing. The Ralushai Report contains a number of cases in which a healer who identified the alleged witch was consulted by elders who only, on their return to the villages, informed their children in order to secure collective participation in the violence. It is by understanding the central role of the elderly in this procedure that the youth-elderly dichotomy in witchcraft violence becomes very questionable.

The case also reveals some of the changes that occurred over time in this domain of witchcraft. Among the Vhavenda witchcraft accusations had been known to emanate from the relatives of the victim to those of the perpetrator, while traditional councils were the ones to try cases of witchcraft and even could impose sentences. However, over the years, the whole community has become involved in witch identification, witchcraft accusations and witch killings. The Ralushai Report revealed that village members from all walks of life participated in the violence against fellow villagers, and that the age of perpetrators ranged from 9 to 59 years. A number of accused were beyond the age of 35, which is an age that does not fall under the youth definition in South Africa, and most countries in the continent. Mkandawire (1996) has shown that the definition of youth age in South Africa is between 15 and 35 years, and that this age together with those of Ghana, Tanzania, Kenya and Mozambique is the highest in Commonwealth countries in Africa.

It is however correct that in the witchcraft violence under discussion there were more old female victims than their male counterparts. However such statistics should not immediately lead to gender categorisation of this witchcraft violence. Rather this statistics should be balanced against other statistics which show that there are more old women than old men in the Province. This is evident in the pension pay-out points in the villages where one finds around 300 old women as compared to around 50 old men.

Political explanations of the witchcraft violence have also recently been questioned. When the Amnesty Committee held hearings in Thohoyandou in an effort to pardon convicts who committed witchcraft murders that were found to have been politically motivated, a number of convicts could not associate themselves with any political organisation of the time. This was despite the fact that they admitted during trial that they committed the crimes while singing struggle songs and even calling one another 'comrades'. In such a witchcraft struggle the reference to 'comrade' and the singing of struggle songs assumed new meaning: they were no longer the reserve of political activists. This time it was acceptable for all involved to sing political songs as long as they showed their determination to rid the countryside of witches. *Comrade* became anyone who was not a witch and who sympathised with the cause of freeing the villages of witches. Researchers also found that

95

"no political organisations seemed overtly or directly involved in the witch-burning [in Venda] during 1990 even though the young people taking part in the witch-hunts used political slogans or wore political T-shirts, and sometimes waved banners and flags of the political organisations… In a number of cases the killings appear to have been spontaneous in that no premeditated or political decision had been taken to kill the suspected witches. Often the youths had intended to expel from the village those allegedly practising witchcraft. However, in certain cases control over the crowd was lost resulting in violent mob attacks on those accused" (Minnaar *et al.*, 1992:49).

If explanations about youth frustrations because of massive unemployment, and comradeship due to party-political association were to be believed, what then would be the explanations offered for the involvement of police in the witchcraft violence? The Ralushai Report found that "in most cases concerning witchcraft or ritual killings, some of the local police secretly try to gain favours by siding with the witch-hunters or people who want to apply instant justice to ritual killers and to the alleged witches… Black policemen also believe in witchcraft and as a result of this belief they are sometimes reluctant to be of any assistance to people having been accused of practicing witchcraft" (Ralushai *et al.*, 1996:62-3). Throughout Apartheid, police in the Venda homeland were notorious for being ruthless when dealing with any politically motivated activity. How then does one account for the sudden turn-about by police in their relationship with the comrades? Moreover, the police service in Venda was then a lucrative and secured profession which most young men and women aspired to join. This renders explanations about unemployment and partisanship not plausible.

It is surprising that the fear of witchcraft has received little attention each time explanations for witchcraft violence were sought. This deliberate avoidance on the part of social scientists may however be understandable given the fact that the focus had initially been on the non-existence of witchcraft despite the prevalence of the witchcraft belief in the studied communities.

Minnaar *et al.*, (1992:42) concluded that "the people in Venda lived in fear – especially fear of witchcraft. The belief in magic, superhuman

96

powers, witches and magic potions cannot be summarily dismissed as superstition. In Venda it is a deeply rooted phenomenon prevalent to a greater or lesser degree among most of the people, even the educated ones. Even those who do not believe in these things can easily fall prey to a medicine murder." It is in such an environment that during violence everyone easily gets mobilised or lends support either in the form of active participation or by donating a certain amount of money in an effort to bail out those behind the murders. The mere fact of knowing that one may become a victim of a witchcraft attack is sufficient to drive a community into a crazy witch hunt. Incidents of witchcraft and ritual murders in political circles in Venda in 1989 resulted in massive school boycotts and student protests. About 3000 students at the University of Venda boycotted classes and also held a protest march to the Thohoyandou police station (Gunene 1989 & Tsedu 1989). Again, these were the youth who were the shining stars, achievers and hopefuls within their communities.

The shortcoming of the modernity theory lies in its sociological approach. Witchcraft, according to this theory, serves as an explanation used by the victims of inexplicable misfortunes that are characteristics of the world economy. The victims are usually from, "the class that suffered most from the poverty, the desperation, the frustration and the helplessness that are a consequence to economic impotence," (Hallen and Sodipo 1986:89). This is indeed, "the weakness of the social disintegration or modernity theory ... it lays too much explanatory power upon change. Change is endemic; so is social disintegration. Conflict between classes (the poor and the rich, the fortunate and the unfortunate) goes on all the time" (Douglas 1999:188).

It is limiting to seek witchcraft explanations by focusing on the ranks of the deprived, unfortunate and marginalized. Witchcraft accusations often circulate within the ranks of the well-off or are, at times, directed at the poor and marginalized by the rich and powerful. This may explain why people involved in the killing of witches in Venda came from all over the kingdom, and their composition was not confined by class, gender, age or party-political identification (Ralushai *et al.*, 1996). During the era of Patrick Ramaano Mphephu (president of the former Venda homeland), accusations of witchcraft were rife in his

97

cabinet, where ministers traded accusations against one another. Chief Frank Ramovha, a deputy minister, was sentenced to death after having been found guilty on a charge of medicine murder. A similar suspicion applied to Andrew Tshivhase who was hanged in 1984 for committing a medicine murder, while his brother, Alfred Tshivhase, was later forced to resign from the cabinet because of persistent rumours of him being involved in medicine murders. The Director-General of Venda's Intelligence Service, Theophillus Mutshaini, was a member of a group of people accused of the medicine murder of an infant (Minnaar *et al.*, 1992:42-3). After his death, Mphephu was rumoured to have been bewitched by one of his cabinet who used *tshiganame* (a certain witchcraft technique) to cause his sudden death.

Postcolonial South Africa is also not free from witchcraft accusations within the ranks of the politically and economically powerful. The story of Kwazulu-Natal's Member of the Executive Council of Education, Faith Gaza, who abandoned her ministerial office and duties for three weeks because she believed that her axed predecessor, Eileen Shandu, was bewitching her, exemplifies this point (*Sunday Times*, 15 October 2000). In such circumstances, the experience and knowledge that people have about witchcraft is sufficient to trigger accusations and violent reactions. Witchcraft accusations and violence, therefore, become an occurrence perpetrated by the fear of witchcraft attack rather than a scapegoat for recurring misfortunes. Bell's (1992:27) insightful remark that, "if the natural world is ruled by fate and chance, and the technical world by rationality and entropy, the social world can only be characterised as existing in fear and trembling" is apt. Although African societies with witchcraft beliefs and practices are found in various localities in Africa, these societies exist in worlds that are engulfed in constant fear resulting from people's experience and knowledge of witchcraft. Surprisingly, these local understandings (experiences and knowledge) of witchcraft are usually ignored when explanations for variations in witchcraft beliefs and actions are sought.

The Apartheid State and witchcraft violence

What then did the Apartheid State have to do with the witchcraft violence that ravaged Venda and other areas of the Limpopo Province? The seminal mistake made by colonial governments throughout Africa was the assumption that outlawing witchcraft would automatically uproot beliefs in the existence of occult forces. In South Africa, the apartheid state side-lined and undermined witchcraft-related institutions. The Witchcraft Suppression Act, passed in 1957, aimed to punish any person who, "professes or pretends to use any supernatural power, witchcraft, sorcery, enchantment or conjuration ... employs or solicits any witchdoctor, witch-finder or any other person to name or indicate any person as a wizard," (No. 3 of 1957, as amended in 1970). The Act declared witchcraft to be a false belief, in contrast to Western rationality, and punished those who accused or divined others as witches rather than those who were said to practice witchcraft or sorcery. It placed witchcraft cases under the jurisdiction of modern courts, thereby retracting the powers that traditional councils had over these cases.

Despite its objective, the Act did not achieve in rooting out the belief in witchcraft. Neither did it help in allaying villager's fear of witchcraft attack. As Tebbe (2007:197) observed "in the perspective of many Africans...traditional techniques of resolving witchcraft disputes have been outlawed while those seen as committing acts of occult aggression have escaped both governmental and traditional punishment... Many people inferred...that the government had sided with witches and was even relying on them to bolster its power."

The three cases described in this chapter demonstrate that among the Vhavenda there are local institutions with the expressed purpose of dealing with witchcraft.

An arena for mediation between the accuser and the accused is also provided for in traditional councils. These courts play a conciliatory role in witchcraft-related cases, thus calming the emotions of both parties until a solution is found, which is aimed at preventing the loss of life. Compared to their modern counterparts, traditional institutions have been relatively successful in dealing with witchcraft. There is a high turnout in these courts, which may be attributed to the participatory approach of the courts, as well as their desire to reconcile antagonists and to rehabilitate offenders. Central to the traditional council is, "the institution of traditional leadership in which customs, traditions and cultural practices form the basis of the legal system that regulates the lives of the people" (Donkers and Murray 1997:39). The institution has both religious and spiritual roles that are familiar to most participants. These functions involve the spiritual powers that are inherent in traditional leadership positions and underlie the reverence with which the leaders are held. Traditional leaders are, "believed to represent ancestors or the legendary founding father of the group and to provide the link between the deities and the people as well as between the living and the dead members of the community who, in traditional cosmology, remain in close communion" (Osaghae 1997:119). It is on this basis that traditional councils are able to regulate witchcraft and the supernatural.

Once these institutions, whose purpose was to deal partly with witchcraft-related matters were incapacitated, the Vhavenda found themselves with no institutions for protection and mediation. The impotency of traditional councils stranded everyone (the witch, the bewitched, traditional leaders and traditional healers) in a witchcraft-ridden environment. On the one hand, the alleged witch was left exposed to the vengeance of his/her would be accusers who, in the absence of an arena for mediated confrontation, would presume him/her guilty and kill him/her. Cases of alleged witches who went to *musanda* (chiefs' place) to report witchcraft accusations became frequent in Venda. These alleged witches were however turned away by chiefs who indicated that the law no longer allowed them to preside over witchcraft cases. On the other hand, the bewitched found himself/herself face to face with the witch who would traumatise him/her (the bewitched) with his/her (the witch's) professed witchcraft with no institutions the bewitched could resort to for help. The Ralushai Report (Ralushai *et al.*, 1996:13) documented a case in which "a [boy] at Dinga village in the Malamulele district was threatened by an old man that he would be struck by lightning on 9 November 1995. Lightning indeed struck the hut in which the threatened boy was sleeping. On Saturday the 11th of the same month, lightning again struck a friend's hut where the same boy had sought refuge."

100

In their courts, chiefs were often accused of having been dishonest to their people and supporting the illegitimate regime. Chiefs were blamed for not defying the law that prohibited them from presiding over witchcraft cases, while they knew that their people were still experiencing witchcraft-related problems. Traditional healers also became villains in their communities. Their refusal to become involved in witchcraft matters did not only cost them their legitimacy in the community, but it was also often said that they were directly or indirectly taking part in witchcraft attacks and ritual murders.

The statutory suppression of witchcraft beliefs meant that witchcraft-related problems were no longer communicated within these communities. Once there was a suspicion of witchcraft at play, people refrained from their usual ways of consultation in order to ascertain the real culprit behind the foul play. Communication between the accused and the accuser was also rendered impossible. Members of community did not want to be seen to be participating in any witchcraft-related activity as everyone was afraid that he/she would be seen as contravening the Act, thereby placing oneself in the hands of the police. Once witchcraft violence broke out, this silence that was a result of fear from persecution became a fuelling factor. Unlike with other crimes where members of these communities got together to expose those who committed them, when witchcraft-related crimes were committed they were met with unbearable silence.

Prohibiting traditional councils from presiding over witchcraft-related cases also made matters worse. It should be noted that in these communities traditional councils are the coordinating agencies of community policing. So, incapacitating these courts on witchcraft-related matters meant that the moral responsibility that every member of these communities had in terms of reporting crimes was eventually lost. The custom has been that once a crime of any nature is committed, such a crime will get reported to *musanda* by any person, either those involved in the crime or those who simply witnessed it. This is taken as the moral duty of every member, and failure to carry this out results in certain punitive steps being taken against the culprit by members of these communities. A messenger would then be dispatched from *musanda* to contact the nearest police station so the police could handle the matter. Conversely, if police are informed that there is a crime committed in a particular community, they would usually first go to *musanda* upon which any member would take them to the spot of the crime.

Once the Act prohibited every member of these communities (chiefs, witches, healers and ordinary villagers) from engaging in witchcraft beliefs and practices, this act of community policing fell away. That moral responsibility to report crimes committed began to exclude witchcraft-related crimes. Chiefs discouraged those who ran to their courts to report witchcraft-related incidents, thus silence over crimes related to this force was sanctioned in these communities. It became common knowledge to every member, even to those who just visited these communities, that community policing still existed but it did not involve witchcraft-related crimes. One should note that the low levels of crime in the villages are much attributed to this community policing that is fostered by traditional authorities. During the witchcraft violence, police would run to the spot of the crime only to be met with non-cooperation from both the chiefs and community members. On probing why people could not cooperate with the police when they came to investigate witchcraft-related crimes, one Mafefe, an old man of around 60s, told me in a *khoro* at Mandiwana that:

"You see my son, there is no crime that is committed within this area that our chief [Mandiwana] is not made aware of, and these police know very much well that we are the ones that inform them of these crimes while they are far away in their police stations. These police, however, have decided that our chief should no longer deal with issues that involve witchcraft. So, now what happens is that people bypass Mandiwana and go straight to the police to report witchcraft related crimes. Then when we are seated in our houses we are surprised by police who come, without the company of any person from the chief's kraal, to ask us about a particular crime that they say has been reported. So, these police expect us to disclose information to them about a crime that our chief is not even aware of. You see my son, we cannot do that, and we cannot tell the police what we know. We do not belong under the police; we are the

102

people of Mandiwana. Even if you check in our documents you will find that they are written we are the subjects of headman Mandiwana and not of the police" [this is followed by a huge applause from the gathering] (pers. comm. 2000).

Such is the context within which witchcraft-related crimes take place. As Donkers and Murray (1997: 41) stated the traditional community can be regarded as a mini-state within the broader state context. Like with other crimes, witchcraft-related crimes give rise to issues concerning boundaries and identity. In these localities of the Limpopo Province, every traditional community has its own domain whose boundaries are known. Most people under the jurisdiction of a traditional authority consider themselves members of that specific community and, according to custom, are accepted and recognised as such. All these are issues that the police consider in dealing with any form of crimes in these communities: the police access crime scenes in these communities through the traditional authority. However, the incapacitation of traditional authorities over witchcraft-related issues, and the police by-pass of these authorities to crime scenes within the jurisdiction of a traditional authority, had only served to alienate the support of traditional authorities and their people in witchcraft-related crimes.

The situation was not made any better by modern courts, which substituted for traditional councils in handling witchcraft cases, because of their failure to allay the fear of witchcraft. From the point of view of witchcraft victims, modern courts protected witches because, unlike traditional councils, they did not allow people to approach them with complaints of being bewitched. In situations such as the above, exasperated communities, which had already lost criminal jurisdiction in their customary law courts in favour of colonial state courts, began to perceive the colonial judge as a strong ally of the witch. The frightening outcome of witchcraft trials was that colonial courts for lack of substantive proof constantly set witches free. Aggrieved parties who took matters into their own hands and attacked witches, either in self-defence or during moments of sheer provocation, were instantly convicted for their acts and harsh sentences were meted out against

103

them by the same colonial courts (Fisiy, 1998:149). Here the refusal by modern courts to integrate local cosmology during criminal trials alienated the courts from these communities.

Modern courts either punished those who confessed to practising witchcraft or dismissed their confessions as pretence. People who confessed to witchcraft were either considered to have been coerced or were seen as suffering from a "depressed personality, a form of personality disorder. Here the tendency was to see the witch as a victim of social forces that are beyond his or her control, an involuntary scapegoat who is forced to confess to excesses that are patently empirically impossible, thereby highlighting in an indirect manner the underlying social problems for which the society must victimise him or her. The witch who confesses voluntarily was seen as a person whose problems cause him or her to become oppressed by so strong a sense of personal guilt that he or she one day confesses to crimes that are morbidly excessive in nature," (Hallen and Sodipo 1986:95-6). By implication, witches were given the right to harm other people, as long as they did not say they were witches before the courts. As a result, the bewitched were plagued by a sense of helplessness in the face of this occult force because when faced with a witchcraft threat, the bewitched could no longer appeal to any institution for either protection or mediation. Coupled with a weakened state in the run up to the transition to a democratic and integrated South Africa, the killing of witches became the bewitched's easy option. The situation started with sporadic incidents of violence that were soon to escalate out of control. Between 1980 and 1997, about 1 000 alleged witches had been killed in former Venda, Lebowa and Gazankulu (now Limpopo Province). Around 300 of these killings occurred between 1990 and 1995 (Mavhungu, 1999:7).

The incapacity of traditional institutions to deal with witchcraft unrest and the reluctance of their modern substitutes to deal with witchcraft matters, and not modernity, are the main explanations for witchcraft violence in the Limpopo Province. In a study on witchcraft violence in the Eastern Province of Cameroon, Geschiere and Fisiy (1994:333) also observed that:

... the [socio-economic] inequalities are more marked in other provinces – for instance, in the West, where there has been increasing land scarcity for several decades. Yet the pressure on the state to intervene in local witchcraft matters seems to be less strong in these areas. What is striking in the Eastern Province, and in other parts of the Cameroonian forest area, is that local societies seem no longer able to generate their own mechanisms for dealing with the growing unrest over witchcraft.

This observation by the two authors is reinforced by regular incidents of alleged witches that escape death from other provinces of Cameroon and seek refuge in the North-West Province. An alleged witch in the North-West is sure of survival as he or she gets ostracised or banished. The same witch is however sure to have his or her fate decided differently in other provinces of Cameroon: the witch may either get killed or, if lucky, escape death with his or her property destroyed. For example, the following incident from Cameroon as reported in The *Herald*, 15 October 2001, will serve to illustrate this point:

"Patrick Ewi escaped lynching in the South West province some years back as he was accused of witchcraft crimes. He sought refuge in Kesu village, Wum in the North-West Province. On his arrival here Patrick was housed by his uncle whom he later killed because of witchcraft. Patrick was recently banished from the village by the highest traditional authority – Kwifoyn – in connection with the death of Caroline Nsen through alleged witchcraft practices. The 33 year old Caroline, wife of Francis Azong, died in September 2001 after having fallen sick for a long time. When the sickness persisted, Francis consulted a traditional healer who told him that Patrick was responsible for the illness. The healer said Francis was to blame because he owed Patrick 400 FCFA. Francis then reported the matter to both the juju and the chief of Kesu. Chief Kangsen reacted by summoning the villagers and the accused, and ordered for further investigation into the illness of Caroline by consulting other healers. Patrick was again confirmed guilty. On returning to the village, Patrick admitted his guilt and further confessed that he was responsible for the death of over seven people in the village. Chief Kangsen then asked Patrick to save Caroline's life at all cost. Patrick then stopped by Francis's home once and was given 500 FCFA for medication. He

also made several attempts to save Caroline's life but all in vain. Caroline died on 24 September. When villagers became aware of Caroline's death, the youths were instructed to bring Patrick to the chief's place. The Kwifoyn then took Patrick and paraded him around the town before taking him towards Befang in Menchum valley. Here he was escorted out of Kesu village and ordered not to return."

The above incident demonstrates the different way in which people in the North-West Province as compared to those from other provinces react to witchcraft incidents. Indeed, there are stark differences between the North-West and other provinces in Cameroon. As demonstrated in chapter 3, the North-West still has its traditional institutions intact; chiefs enjoy full legitimacy and still deal with most customary matters including witchcraft, with relative success. This "well institutionalised point" is lacking in other provinces, and may explain why youth in Kom consider witchcraft matters to be beyond their competence, and thus falling within the exclusive domain of the elders. This situation exists despite the fact that socio-economic inequities are more acute in Kom, and unemployment among the youth has rocketed high, at a scale incomparable to that of Venda.

In their study of witchcraft in Cameroon, Geschiere and Nyamnjoh (1998:87) observed that traditional leaders were the obvious figures to appeal to [by witchcraft believers in both the urban and rural areas] when witchcraft seemed to be proliferating amongst them. Niehaus (2001:190) also argued that evidence from the Lowveld in South Africa showed "a definite correlation between the non-recognition of witchcraft and the advent of witch-killings. Hardly any killings occurred when chiefs acted in consonance with the expectations of villagers by mediating in witchcraft accusations. The accuser's desire for vengeance was dissipated through alternatives forms of punishment, and they were afforded the opportunity of being compensated for their misfortunes. At the same time those accused of witchcraft were given a chance to prove their innocence, and were provided with protection."

The Ralushai Report had also touched on the life-saving intervention of traditional authorities on witchcraft matters. In the case where the boy who was threatened with lightning by the old man survived the lightning strike twice, "the following day the community met at the headman's kraal were both incidents were discussed. The name of the old man was mentioned. It was decided that the old man should leave the area" (Ralushai *et al.*, 1996:13). During the witchcraft violence, the man lived under police protection at Malamulele.

Conclusion

The existence of local mechanisms to contain witchcraft and the impact that state policies have on these local structures may go further in explaining the variations of witchcraft beliefs and actions over time. It is no co-incidence that the period after the inauguration of the democratic government was met with the decline in the killing of witches. This is despite the fact that the modernity project is still in progress, acute socio-economic inequities are peaking, and unemployment amongst the youth is on the increase. The decline in witchcraft violence can be attributed to the new openness that was created since 1994. In addition to government's policy that recognized traditional healers, traditional councils took advantage of the leniency shown by the new government towards traditional institutions. As evident in the above cases, traditional councils, as well as family gatherings, started to try cases of witchcraft (even though it was to a limited extent).

The three cases presented in this chapter demonstrate that while witchcraft accusations may frequently be accompanied by feelings of envy, jealousy and hatred, the knowledge and experience that people have about witchcraft is sufficient to trigger an accusation and violent reaction. The fear of witchcraft is common amongst the believers and is therefore not something to dismiss lightly. This fear, when not well managed, has the potential to cause believers to harm and murder people accused of being witches regardless of any facts or circumstances surrounding the accusations.

Chapter Five

Policy Options for Post-Colonial South Africa

Introduction

The preceding chapters are concerned with the broader context within which this research was undertaken: the theoretical perspectives and literature on witchcraft; the comparison of witchcraft beliefs and practices, the containment of witchcraft in Kom and Venda; and the implication that this study has for anthropological theories. This chapter broadly examines some of the lessons drawn from the study with the intention of enhancing the ongoing policymaking process on witchcraft in South Africa. Amid the increasing calls for the postcolonial South African state to redress the past injustices brought about by its apartheid predecessor in the occult domain, what are the policy options available to the legislators? Should they opt for an easy route and uphold the status quo which constitutes the legal suppression of witchcraft or should they give in to calls for the recognition and criminalisation of witchcraft? An argument is made that the Witchcraft Suppression Act of 1957, as amended in 1970, should be completely repealed and not substituted by a law that recognises and seeks to control witchcraft, as suggested by witchcraft believers.

Suppressing witchcraft beliefs and practices

As illustrated earlier in this book, the colonial response to witchcraft-related challenges in Africa was to deny the existence of witchcraft, to punish witchcraft accusers and anyone who professed to have knowledge of witchcraft. It was held that not only would this make witchcraft gradually disappear but it would also protect the innocent victims of witchcraft accusations. The Ralushai Report stated that "in 1895 when the first Witchcraft Suppression Act was

109

passed in the Cape of Good Hope, the legislature made it clear in the Act that, although certain people may genuinely believe in witchcraft, it regarded the whole practice of witchcraft as a pretence and a sham, something which in actual fact has no real existence at all" (Ralushai *et.al.*, 1996:54).

It was within the context of such denial that, throughout Africa, legislation suppressing witchcraft was enacted. In South Africa, the Witchcraft Suppression Act of 1957 was based on a similar colonial-era statute of the Cape Colony referred to above. The implementation of the Act by the Apartheid State, as Niehaus (2001:184) argued "gave symbolic expression to the civilising mission of colonialism. The law demanded no compromise in any belief or practice pertaining to witchcraft. These were perceived as baseless and even as diabolic primitive superstitions that had to be suppressed and eliminated through education, Christian proselytisation and the spread of Western civilisation."

The conviction in the non-existence of witchcraft was not only limited to policymakers but was also shared by policy practitioners, anthropologists and other social scientists. Winter (1963), who was regarded as an authority on witchcraft in Africa, once stated, "there is no reason to think that anyone does in fact practise witchcraft or even that anyone could practise it." Later Lewis (1976) declared, "I certainly do not believe in witchcraft. I make this declaration because…we do not need to share other people's beliefs in order to understand them sympathetically: We can see sense in beliefs even when we are convinced they are based on false premises."

The previous chapter recognised that the democratic South African Government still uses the Witchcraft Suppression Act of 1957 to police witchcraft. The law attempts to stamp out the belief in witchcraft by criminalising virtually all witchcraft-related conduct, including accusing anyone of practising witchcraft, engaging in divination techniques designed to detect witches, and the [pretended] practice of witchcraft itself. Critically, the 1957 Act effectively prohibits all forms of private policing because it bans divination, which is the only recognised technique for detecting witches (Tebbe, 2007:197).

Throughout the Act, there is a persistent denial of the reality of witchcraft. Hence it is not the practice of witchcraft that is criminalised. Rather, it is "pretend[ing] to use witchcraft," "profess[ing] a knowledge of witchcraft" or "supply[ing] any person with any pretended means of witchcraft." Consequently, levelling witchcraft accusations at any other person is criminal, so is the act of identifying witches by a 'witchdoctor' or witch-finder'. The concept of burden of proof is irrelevant. Those who lay charges are not afforded the chance to provide evidence as the matter under dispute is already legally assumed non-existent. Similarly, those who confess to engaging in witchcraft practice are prosecuted and sentenced for claiming to have committed an imaginary act without being given the opportunity to prove their culpability.

Generally the Act outlaws making witchcraft accusations against anyone. The logic is that accusations are punishable as they are often associated with violence towards alleged witches. However, just like other cases, witchcraft accusations should not constitute an offence if the accuser can prove the bases on which the allegations are made. The law does not consider this because its authors did not believe witchcraft existed.

This explains the perception by witchcraft believers that instead of protecting innocent civilians from the constant attacks of witches, the Act sides with witches and even shelters them from any other form of punishment. Meanwhile accused witches also learnt that the law did little to protect them. The law instead achieved the opposite by driving witchcraft belief and accusations underground which in turn resulted in communities resorting to vigilantism – as it was seen in Venda – as a method of self-defence. Accused witches were subjected to constant harassment, ostracisation, banishment, violence and death.

The Act is also viewed as denigrating African cultural beliefs and practices. It implies that any person accused of practising witchcraft is a 'wizard'. This is considered discriminatory in that amongst the believers, a 'wizard' is not understood to be an all-embracing concept for a witch but is instead a reference in the literature to a male person who practices witchcraft.

The Act makes reference to a 'witch-doctor' or witch-finder'. The use of these names is defamatory in that this refers to traditional healers, generally specialists in traditional medicine in their communities. As Ashforth (2005: 138-39) observed "many Africans supported the change [from witch-doctor to traditional healer] because they felt that the term [witch-doctor] wrongly associated healing with witchcraft – a connection that they found insulting – and because they felt that the colonial term harkened back to a general disrespect for African traditions."

The South African Parliament' Select Committee on Social Services reported that healers felt aggrieved that their practice was outlawed by the Witchcraft Suppression Act. They felt "degraded and dehumanised by such laws, which not only communicated state opprobrium, but also had the effect of associating healers with witches in the eyes of the public" (Tebbe, 2007:219). While legislators sought to address the grievances of traditional healers by passing the Traditional Health Practitioners Act in 2004, this was insufficient as the Witchcraft Suppression Act remains in force.

The Act should be completely repealed as it is unconstitutional. It violates the Bill of Rights which is contained in The Constitution of the Republic of South Africa, 1996. The Act is at odds with the sections of the Constitution which guarantee everyone 'the right to freedom of conscience, religion, thought, belief and opinion; the right to participate in the cultural life of their choice, the right to enjoy their culture and practise their religion'. Keeping this Act in existence therefore violates the rights of believers and is in contradiction with the Constitution. It can therefore be argued that South Africans have the right to believe in witchcraft. Besides, there are many other beliefs, in the 'Rainbow Nation', that are not criminalised. In line with the Constitution, South African laws should be neutral towards beliefs. The belief in witchcraft should be viewed as unproblematic, and any associated human right abuse or violence should be dealt with under general criminal law.

Recognising the reality of witchcraft

As demonstrated throughout this book, witchcraft is an experiential reality and a real human problem in both Kom and Venda. Suppressive witchcraft policies throughout Africa did not bring about the desired consequences. To the contrary, the belief in witchcraft is prevalent and is not showing signs of diminishing. "Witchcraft belief and experience are deeply rooted in Africa. There can be no question of denying or ignoring this fact. The impact weighs heavily on society," so observed Father Tatar Mbuy, the diocesan priest of the archdiocese of Bamenda, North West Province of Cameroon (Mbuy, 1989).

In South Africa, the Ralushai Report made a similar observation: "the belief in witchcraft is deep-rooted and that it has become very clear that no one can argue that witchcraft is a myth which can only exist in the minds of the ignorant" (Ralushai et al, 1996: 56). A few years later, Douglas (1999) remarked that the Lele of Kasai region in the Democratic Republic of Congo still had both the belief in and the fear from the attack of witchcraft despite the fact that the Belgian colonialists did everything to incapacitate those institutions that the Lele had put in place to detect, disable and punish witches.

Anthropological studies have recently provided explanations on the persistence of the belief in witchcraft in Africa. They reveal that the belief in witchcraft represents the African expression of the devil and morality. Hence contrary to the modernist argument that the enlightened African will stop believing in witchcraft, this belief is held by amongst others the educated, the middle class, the rich, bureaucrats, politicians, and religious leaders (Fisiy, 1998; Geschiere and Nyamnjoh, 1998; Meyer, 1998; and Douglas, 1999; amongst others).

Indeed, witchcraft is no longer a belief exclusive to the heathens or a residue of the primitive culture. The belief in witchcraft is as pervasive amongst church goers as it is amongst those outside the Christian faith. It is used by charismatic Christian religious leaders as a manifest form of satanic evil. Church-goers are constantly encouraged to find (accuse) and convert suspected witches. The result is that the notion of Satanism is incorporated into more traditional beliefs around witchcraft. The Roman Catholic Church, the most influential Christian denomination in Malawi, has stated that witchcraft is real and that it is investigating solutions to the problems of witchcraft for its followers (South African Pagan Rights Alliance, 2010).

During fieldwork, it was observed that witchcraft is a real belief system that is rooted in the popular mentality of many Cameroonians and South Africans. Such is a social reality that decision-makers are increasingly called to address. As has been evident with the postcolonial South African State, most States in Africa, unlike their colonial predecessors, are not that preoccupied with whether or not witchcraft is a reality or a mirage. Their concern is that witchcraft is a serious policy problem that requires urgent attention. Geschiere (1997: 216) noted that "the colonial authorities were primarily intent on containing manifestations of witchcraft (or anti-witchcraft): their overriding concern was to maintain law and order. Postcolonial authorities, in contrast, are much more sensitive to the popular pressure to intervene against what is perceived as an unprecedented spread of witchcraft."

Both the witchcraft commission and the national conference on witchcraft in South Africa are clear efforts by the postcolonial South African state to intervene in the occult domain. They are a response to popular calls to the State to criminalise the practice of witchcraft, a policy attempt that represents a new approach that holds within it the respect for the beliefs that members of these communities have in relation to mystical power. This perspective sees a belief in witchcraft as neither irrational nor as a resort to explain certain phenomenon, be it modernity or otherwise, but as part of the religious corpus of African beliefs. The government is expected to acknowledge, as Mbiti (1990:197) argues, that "whatever reality there is concerning witchcraft in the broad and popular sense of the term, the belief in it is there in African [communities], and that belief affects everyone, for better or for worse." It is clear that the postcolonial mind-set with regard to witchcraft is completely different from that which prevailed during the colonial era. The Witchcraft Suppression Act should

114

therefore be repealed. However, as it shall be shown below, the recognition of the reality of witchcraft should not necessarily lead to the introduction of a new law that criminalises the act of bewitching.

Criminalising witchcraft practice

The South African state is implored to recognise the reality of witchcraft and criminalise the practice of witchcraft. This, it is argued, will enable the state to control rather than suppress this rampant occult force. It will allay the fears of its citizens and will increase the perceived legitimacy of the government. The move will also mark the recognition of African belief systems, thus further strengthening legitimacy of the law with regard to its congruence with the beliefs of the people.

It is proposed that the new law should provide for the control of the practice of witchcraft and similar practices. The law should make it an offence for any person who "does any act which creates a reasonable suspicion that he (she) is engaged in the practice of witchcraft" (Ralushai *et.al.*, 1996:55). From the ontological point of view, it is hard to imagine how such suspicion can be reasonably proven in a court of law. Witchcraft is a supernatural act, unobservable and undetectable by ordinary methods, and therefore impossible to prove in a reasonable way. The unreasonableness surrounding witchcraft lies in its accusations which can simply be triggered by confessions of children; occurrence of diseases such as HIV/Aids, misfortunes such as a car accident, natural disaster such as storm or famine, and the presence of witchcraft familiars such as a hyena, *tokoloshi*, baboon, black cat, snake, owl; wildcat and lightning bird. Criminalisation of witchcraft practice will result in a plethora of cases for which the courts will find it impossible to obtain evidence.

After analysing a multitude of cases and listening to testimony relating to witchcraft incidents, the Ralushai Report noted "the most vexing problem surrounding witchcraft is that the activities of a witch cannot be witnessed by naked eyes. This means that one cannot be in a position to say that a witch has done this and that. It is clear that eye witnesses are not available in cases involving witchcraft except for those few cases where people are caught naked inside someone's yard" (Ralushai *et.al.*, 1996:57). Criminalising witchcraft may amount to the State outlawing ghosts. While the belief in witchcraft is prevalent, there is barely any evidence that witches exist. Even people who claim to have the supernatural powers to manipulate events to cause other people ill, harm or to die have difficulties in demonstrating that the attributes of witches are true.

Similarly, the Malawi Law Commission – in reviewing the witchcraft law of that country – observed that through normal legal procedures, the vexing issue of providing evidence from witchcraft arises. Witchcraft, at its core, involves the use of supernatural or non-natural powers and is therefore undetectable by ordinary methods and impossible to prove in any principled way (Malawi Law Commission, 2009). The issue of evidence will therefore become a challenge to the South African courts if witchcraft practice is to be criminalised. Claims on witchcraft will remain unsubstantiated and evidence will not be verifiable in courts.

Byrne (2011:2) observes, "the phenomenon is further exacerbated by a strong belief that the ability to identify suspected witches is held exclusively by traditional healers through various methods of divination – who are then afforded the right to identify as well as cleanse suspected witches through the administering of traditional medicine and other harmful cleansing rituals."

Indeed as it was demonstrated in chapter 3, healers play a central role in the identification, charging and conviction of witches. Of concern for modern courts should be that "divinatory techniques only make sense within a particular comprehensive viewpoint. Proposals to criminalise witchcraft therefore violate the Rawlsian criterion of reciprocity: they cannot be accepted by reasonable people who are not adherents of that culture. Methods that traditional healers use to detect the secret practice of sorcery necessarily involve supernatural practices whose logic is opaque to observers. Divination involves just the sort of governmental arbitrariness prohibited by virtually all versions of the rule of law (Tebbe, 2007:234).

Fisiy and Geschiere (1990) have observed that in convicting witches, the Cameroonian courts rely in such cases on the testimony

116

of 'modern' certificated 'witch-doctors' who operate in an uneasy alliance with the state. They expressed strong reservations about this process in which individuals are heavily fined and jailed on the basis of such testimony while protesting their innocence. If the witchcraft practice was to be criminalised, the South African state would risk similar victimisation and discrimination of suspected witches. The courts would be confronted with supernatural evidence they could do nothing about. Healers would present divinatory evidence that court officers could neither comprehend not interpret. They would inform the courts of messages from the ancestors that no other person could attest to.

To the believers, modern courts are not the appropriate location where cases relating to the occult can be heard. Witches are known not to be ordinary people: they are manipulators of circumstances. They have the supernatural power to blind decision-makers so that the verdict goes their way even when it is not supposed to. Before a case is heard, witches perform witchcraft rituals to ensure that those involved in the case may not be able to comprehend the extent of their wrongdoing. The healer, who is a constant presence in traditional councils, helps neutralize this malevolent power of witches.

The absence of a healer in modern courts constitutes a weak link in the perceived ability of these courts to deal witchcraft cases fairly and in a justified manner. Decisions of modern courts over witchcraft-related cases lack legitimacy because presiding officers are viewed as unfit for cases of this nature. Here, one is faced with issues of a clear cultural divergence. In the Western sense, modern courts provide for a neutral venue where both parties can be heard without the fear of intimidation. The judge or the magistrate embodies impartiality: he or she views the facts of the case objectively and rationally without being influenced by his or her preconceived ideas. Both the accused and the accuser are deemed equal before the "White Man's" law. However, when it comes to witchcraft, the threat to security is not always visible, and equality before the law can be subverted by one's unfair access to supernatural powers. The only impartial venue that can strip the feuding parties of their magical

117

influences, and leave them to be judged based on the merit of evidence at their disposal is a traditional council that is protected by a healer.

In demonstrating the inability of the courts to contain a treacherous force such as witchcraft, Geschiere and Nyamnjoh (1998:88) argued that the "Cameroonian state's judicial interventions against witchcraft in the East Province have been most ineffective and even counterproductive. The state with its prisons and gendarmes may possess an impressive disciplinary apparatus, but it is utterly incapable of neutralising the witches' dangerous power." Also on the same issue, Fisiy (1998: 144) wrote, "witchcraft in Cameroon couldn't be dealt with in modern courts. Witchcraft practices are perceived to fall within the domain of the occult powers that are considered as defining a major part of the cosmology and belief system of local population in Africa. Hence in Cameroon, courts still depend on evidence provided for by traditional healers and community members. The courts' reliance on the institution of traditional healing for evidence is understandable since it is very difficult to establish proof on matters involving occult practices."

Geschiere and Nyamnjoh (1998) further cautioned the new controversial role of traditional healers in which "the nganga, the expert of old on the subject of containing witchcraft, becomes a disciplinary figure who drags his suspects before the gendarmes, rather than a healer who is able to neutralise their dangerous force." As Fisiy (1998:144) further argues "the homogenizing role of criminal law – by applying a common frame of legal reference to all citizens – does not necessarily produce a unifying framework for citizenship. [Thus] any attempt to establish proof [over these occult cases] in court which is de-linked from local understandings of the alleged practices will further alienate the people from the court system and widen the chasm between the state and its subjects."

Conclusion

In this chapter it has been argued that the South African state cannot hope to contain witchcraft-related violence by having a law

118

that either suppresses or seeks to control witchcraft. It was pointed out that legislating against witchcraft neither succeeded in eradicating its beliefs and practices nor preventing witchcraft-related violence. In most instances, the violence escalated and a sense of lawlessness crept in. It is further contended that recognising the reality of witchcraft by criminalising the act of bewitching may not help communities feel protected from the constant attacks of witches. Not only will this approach drag the state into mediating disputes relating to the complex and contested realm of the supernatural, it will risk compromising a liberal democratic state's ability to ensure free and fair justice to all its citizens. As Niehaus (2001:193) concluded, in the contexts in which witchcraft beliefs are held "the law may well be more of an irrelevance than a decisive influence."

On its part the state can discourage witchcraft-related violence not by legally isolating witchcraft as a crime but by punishing these violent acts generally within its criminal justice system. The belief in witchcraft and the influence it plays in the commission of crimes, just like any other belief, can be left to the courts to consider when dealing with cases. Accommodating beliefs in court proceedings will pose little risk to the democratic project of the 'Rainbow nation'. As Tebbe (2007:183) indicated, "common law accommodation... maintains the basic universalism of the criminal law, recognising African traditions only at the level of interpretation and application of general rules. Judges reduce sentences for occult-related crimes only by applying legal concepts that apply to everyone regardless of religion or culture, such as culpable homicide, extenuating circumstance, and even blameworthiness. Easing burdens on criminal defendants by applying those categories retains the authority of the general legal framework and risks relatively little division among the citizenry."

The Ralushai Report contained numerous cases which revealed that South African criminal courts have been accommodating witchcraft beliefs in sentencing accused who committed violence or murders while holding a belief of the occult force. In the Netshiavha V The State case in 1990, the Appeal Court concluded that "even though Naledzani [Netshiavha] might be said to have acted

119

negligently [by killing Jim Nephalama], belief in witchcraft is subjective, and in the circumstances, the sentence imposed by the learned judge [of the Venda Supreme Court] was altered from ten to four years imprisonment" (Ralushai *et.al.*, 1996:192).

Accommodating witchcraft beliefs in criminal cases will however not appease the believers of witchcraft who still feel that the State is insensitive to their concerns and failing to protect them from occult aggression. They will still maintain that "supernatural injustice deserves the same sort of state response as ordinary injustice does" (Ashforth, 2005:17). They will argue that giving lenient sentences to people who are seen as freeing their communities of witches does not provide the needed security to villagers. The calls will persist therefore for "parliament to do more to assure people that the government is sensitive to their feelings of vulnerability to the occult" (Tebbe, 2007:183). The role of government is however not to appease a sector of its society at the expense of the broader national project. The government is entrusted with the responsibility to protect, at all cost, the constitutional democracy which is grounded in the ideal of a united, non-racial and non-sexist South Africa.

Bibliography

Abrahams, R. 1994. "Introduction" In R. Abrahams (ed.) *Witchcraft in Contemporary Tanzania*, pp. 9-22. Cambridge: African Studies Centre.

Achebe, C. 1958. *Things Fall Apart*. London: Heinemann.

Anderson, J. 1994 *Public Policymaking*, 2.ed. Boston: Houghton Mifflin Company.

Ashforth, A. 2005. *Witchcraft, Violence and Democracy in South Africa*. Chicago: University of Chicago Press.

Baholo, K. R. 1994. *A Pictorial Response to Certain Witchcraft Beliefs within Northern Sotho Communities*. MFA Thesis, University of Cape Town.

Bell, D. 1992. *Risk Society: Towards a New Modernity*, trans. Ritter, M. London: Sage.

Boddy, J. 1989. *Wombs and Alien Spirits: Women, Men and the Zar Cult in Northern Sudan*. Madison: University of Wisconsin Press.

Bogdanor, V. 1987 *The Blackwell Encyclopaedia of Political Institutions*. New York: Basil Blackwell.

Bolaji, I. 1973. *African Traditional Religion: A Definition*. London: SCM Press.

Booysen, S. and E. Erasmus. 1998. "Public Policy Making in South Africa" in Venter (ed.) *Government and politics in the new South Africa*. Pretoria: Van Schaik.

Burgess, R.G. 1982. *Field Research: A Source Book and Field Manual.* London: Allen & Unwin.

Byrne, C. *Hunting the Vulnerable: Witchcraft and the Law in Malawi.* Consultancy Africa Intelligence, 16 June 2011, http://www.consultancyafrica.com.

Campbell, S.S. 1998. *Called to heal: Traditional healing meets modern medicine in southern Africa today.* Johannesburg: Zebra.

Castetter, W.B. and R. Heisler. 1977. *Developing and defining a dissertation proposal.* Philadelphia: University of Pennsylvania.

Chavunduka, G. 1982. "Witches, Witchcraft and the law in Zimbabwe." *ZINATHA Occasional Papers 1.* Harare. ZINATHA.

---------------------------- 1986. "ZINATHA: The Organization of Traditional Medicine in Zimbabwe." in. M. Last and G. Chavunduka (ed). *The professionalization of African Medicine.* Manchester: Manchester University Press.

Comaroff, J. and J.L. Comaroff. 1997. "Occult economies and the violence of abstraction: notes from the South African postcolony." In: *American Ethnologist.* 26 (2), pp. 279-303.

Comaroff, J. 1994. "Contentious Subjects: Moral beings in the Modern World." In: *Suomen Antropologi* 19, pp. 2-17.

Crawford, J.R. 1967. *Witchcraft and Sorcery in Rhodesia.* Oxford: Oxford University Press.

Creswell, J. 1994. *Research Design: Qualitative & Quantitative Approaches.* Thousand Oaks: Sage.

Dauskardt, R.P.A. 1990. "Traditional medicine: Perspectives and policies in health care development." In: *Development in Southern Africa*, 7(3), pp. 351-358.

Dederen, J.M. 1995. *Killing is easier than paperwork…. A Critique of the Report of the Commission of Inquiry into Witchcraft Violence and Ritual Murders in the Limpopo Province of the Republic of South Africa.* Paper presented to the PAA/AASA Conference. Pretoria: University of South Africa.

Donkers, A. and R. Murray. 1997. "Prospects and Problems Facing Traditional Leaders in South Africa." In: B. De Villiers (ed.). *The Rights of Indigenous People: A Quest for Co-existence.* Pretoria: HSRC Publishers.

Douglas, M. 1999. "Sorcery Accusations Unleashed: The Lele Revisited, 1987." In: *Africa* 69 (2), pp. 177-193.

Dunn, W.N. 1994. *Public Policy Analysis: An Introduction.* New Jersey: Prentice Hall.

Englund, H. 1996. "Witchcraft, Modernity and the Person: the Morality of Accumulation in Central Malawi." In: *Critique of Anthropology* 16 (3), pp. 257-79.

Evans-Pritchard, E.E. 1929. "The Morphology and Function of Magic: A Comparative Study of Trobriand and Zande Ritual and Spells." In: *American Anthropologist* (31), pp. 203-225.

--------------------------- 1935. "Witchcraft." In: *Africa viii* (4), pp 417-422.

--------------------------- 1937. *Witchcraft, Oracles and Magic among the Azande.* London: Oxford University Press.

Fanso, V.G. 1989. *Cameroon History For Secondary Schools and Colleges.* London: Macmillan Education.
123

Fisiy, C.F. 1998. "Containing Occult Practices: Witchcraft Trials in Cameroon." In: *African Studies Review* 41 (3), pp. 143-163.

Fisiy, C.F. and P. Geschiere. 1990. "Judges and Witches, or How is the State to Deal with Witchcraft?" In: *Cahiers d' Etudes Africaines* 118 (30), pp. 135-156.

Foster, D. 1989. *Differences between traditional and modern healers in South Africa.* Berkeley: University of California Press.

Foxcroft, G. 2009. *Witchcraft Accusations: A Protection Concern for UNHCR and the Wider humanitarian Community.* Stepping Stones Nigeria, http://www.crin.org.

Freeman, M. 1995. *Traditional healers in health care in South Africa: A proposal.* The Centre for Health Policy, Department of Community Health, University of the Witwatersrand, Johannesburg.

Freeman, M. and M. Motsei. 1990. *Is There a Role for Traditional Healers in Health Care in South Africa?* The Centre for Health Policy, Department of Community Health, University of the Witwatersrand, Paper No. 20, Johannesburg, March.

Geschiere, P. 1997. *The Modernity of Witchcraft: Politics and the Occult in Postcolonial Africa.* London: University Press of Virginia.

Geschiere, P. and C. Fisiy. 1994. "Domesticating Personal Violence: Witchcraft, Courts and Confessions in Cameroon." In: *Africa* 64 (3), pp. 323-340.

Geschiere, P. and F. Nyamnjoh. 1998. "Witchcraft as an Issue in the "Politics of Belonging": Democratisation and Urban Migrants' Involvement with the Home Village." In: *African Studies Review* 41 (3), pp. 69-91.

Good, C.M. 1987. *Ethnomedical Systems in Africa. Patterns of Traditional Medicine in Rural and Urban Kenya.* New York: Guilford Press.

---------------------------- 1988. "Traditional Healers and AIDS Management in Africa." In: M. Miller & R. Rockwell (eds) *AIDS in Africa: The Social Impact.* New York: Mellon Press.

Green, E.C. 1988. "Can Collaborative Programs Between Biomedical and African Indigenous Health Practitioners Succeed?" In: *Soc. Sci. & Med.,* 27(11), pp. 1125-1130.

---------------------------- 1994. *Aids and STDs in Africa: Bridging the Gap Between Traditional Healing and Modern Medicine.* Pietermaritzburg: University of Natal Press.

Green, R.M. 1983. "Religion and Morality in the African Traditional Setting" In: *Journal of Religion in Africa* XIV (1), pp. 14-28.

Guba, E.G. and Y.S. Lincoln. 1981. *Effective Evaluation.* San Francisco: Jossey-Bass.

Gunene, V. 1989. "Venda in Turmoil after Ritual Deaths." *Weekly Mail,* 28 July.

Hallen, B. and J.O. Sodipo. 1986. *Knowledge, Belief and Witchcraft: Analytic Experiments in African Philosophy.* London: Ethnographica.

Hammersley, M. 1990. *Reading Ethnographic Research: A critical Guide.* London: Longman.

Harnischfeger, J. 2000. "Witchcraft and the State in South Africa." In: *Anthropos* 95, pp. 99-112.

Hiltunen, M. 1986. *Witchcraft and Sorcery in Ovambo.* Finland: The Finnish Anthropological Society.

125

Holland, H. 2001. *African Magic: Traditional Ideas that Heal a Continent.* Johannesburg: Penguin Books.

Kaberry, P.M. 1952. *Women of the Grassfields.* Colonial Office. HMSO, London.

Karp, I. 1995. "African Systems of Thought." In: P.M. Martin and P. O' Meara (eds). *Africa*, pp. 211-22. Bloomington: Indiana University Press.

Kotze, H.J. 1997. *Culture, Ethnicity and Religion: South African Perceptions of Social Identity.* Konrad-Adenauer-Stiftung Occasional Papers. April. RSA: Johannesburg.

Kruschke, E.R. and B.M. Jackson. 1987. *The Public Policy Dictionary.* Oxford: ABC-Clio.

Leininger, M. 1985. "Nature, Rationale, and Importance of Qualitative Methods in Nursing." In: M. Leininger (ed.). *Qualitative Research Methods in Nursing.* Orlando, Fla: Grune& Stratton.

Levy-Bruhl, L. 1926. *how Natives Think.* London: Allen and Unwin.

Lewis, M. 1976. *Social Anthropology in Perspective.* Harmonies-worth: Penguin Books.

Mabogo, D.E.N. 1990. *The Ethnobotany of the Vhavenda.* M.Sc. Unpublished Thesis. University of Pretoria.

MacFarlane, A. 1971. *Witchcraft in Tudor and Stuart England: a regional and comparative study.* London: Routledge & Keegan Paul.

Malan, T. and P.S. Hattingh. 1976. *Black Homelands in South Africa.* Pretoria: Africa Institute of South Africa.

Malawi Law Commission. *Witchcraft Act Review Programme (Issue Paper)*. April 2009, http://www.lawcom.mw.

Martin, P. M. and P. O'Meara. 1995. *Africa*. Bloomington: Indiana University Press.

Marwick, M. G. 1958. "Another modern anti-witchcraft movement in East Central Africa." In: *Africa xxii* (2), pp. 100-112.

---------------------------- 1970. "Sorcery as a Social Strain-Gauge." In: M. Marwick (ed.). *Witchcraft and Sorcery: Selected Readings*. Harmondsworth: Penguin.

Mavhungu, K.N. 1998. *The Policy-Making on a Health Issue: Traditional Healing in South Africa*. M.Phil. Unpublished Thesis. University of Stellenbosch.

---------------------------- 1999. "Heroes, Villains and the State in South Africa's Witchcraft Zone." In: *CONTEXT: Journal of Social and Cultural Studies* 3 (2), pp. 1-21.

Mbiti, J.S. 1969. *African Religions and Philosophy*. London: Heinemann.

Mbuy, T.H. 1989. *Encountering Witches and Wizards in Africa*. Buea, Cameroon.

McCall, J.C. 1995. "Social Organization in Africa." In: P.M. Martin and P. O'Meara (eds). *Africa*, pp. 175-89. Bloomington: Indiana University Press.

McLean, I. 1996. *The Concise Oxford Dictionary of Politics*. Oxford: Oxford University Press.

Merriam, S.B. and E.L. Simpson. 1984. *Guide to Research for Educators and Trainers of Adults*. Malabar: Krieger Publishing Company.

Merriam, S.B. 1991 *Case study research in education: A qualitative approach.* San Francisco: Jossey-Bass.

Meyer, B. 1998. "The Power of Money: Politics, Occult Forces, and Pentecostalism in Ghana." In: *African Studies Review* 41 (3), pp. 15-37.

Mihalik, J. and Y. Cassim. 1992. "Ritual Murder and Witchcraft: A political Weapon." In: *South African Law Journal* 3, p. 138.

Minnaar, A.de V., D. Offrings and C. Payze. 1992. *To Live in Fear: Witchburning and Medicine Murder in Venda.* Pretoria: Human Science Research Council.

Mkandawire, R.M. 1996. *Training Programs for Youth in Commonwealth Africa: Is there a room for a Girl Child?* A document for the Commonwealth Youth Programme Africa Centre.

Mönnig, H. O. 1978. *The Pedi.* Pretoria: Van Schaik.

Moore, H. L. and T Sanders. 2001. *Magical Interpretations, Material Realities: Modernity, Witchcraft and the Occult in postcolonial Africa.* London: Routledge.

Moskovitz, S. 1997. "The Role of Traditional Healers." Orion Medical Management. University of Cape Town.

Motshekga, M.S. 1984. "The Ideology Behind Witchcraft and the Principle of Fault in Criminal Law." In: *Codicillvs* xxxv (2), pp. 4-14.

Ndou, V. P. 1992. *Witchcraft and Witchcraft Accusations: An Analysis of Some Venda Cases of Witchcraft.* Thohoyandou. University of Venda.

Nichols, P. 2000. *Social Survey Methods: A Fieldguide for Development Workers.* Oxford: Oxford GB.

Niehaus, I.A. 1997. "A Witch Has No Horn: The Subjective Reality of Witchcraft in the South African Lowveld" In: *Culture and the Commonplace: Anthropological Essays in Honour of David Hammond-Tooke.* Johannesburg: Witwatersrand University Press.

---------------------------- 1998. "The ANC's Dilemma: The Symbolic Politics of Three Witch-Hunts in the South African Lowveld, 1990-1995." In: *African Studies Review* 41 (3), pp. 93-118.

--------------------------- 1998. *Witchcraft in the New South Africa: From Colonial Superstition to Postcolonial Reality.* Paper presented to the Department of Anthropology at the Witwatersrand University, Johannesburg.

------------------------- 2001. *Witchcraft, Power and Politics: Exploring the Occult in the South African Lowveld.* London: Pluto Press.

Nkwi, P.N. 1976. *Traditional Government and Social Change: A study of the political institutions among the Kom of the Cameroon Grassfields.* Fribourg: The University Press.

---------------------------- 1997. "Rethinking the Role of Elites in Rural Development: A Case Study From Cameroon." In: *Journal of Contemporary African Studies* 15 (1), pp. 67-86.

Nyamnjoh, F.B. 1997. "Political Rumour in Cameroon." In: *Cahier UCAC* 2, pp. 93-105.

Osaghae, E. 1997. "The Role and Functions of Traditional Leaders and Indigenous Groups in Nigeria." In: B. De Villiers (ed.). *The Rights of Indigenous People: A Quest for Co-existence.* Pretoria: HSRC Publishers.

Owens, R.G. 1982. "Methodological Rigor in Naturalistic Inquiry: Some issues and Answers." In: *Educational Administration Quarterly* 18 (2), pp. 2-21.

Patton, M.Q. 1985. *Quality in Qualitative Research: Methodological Principles and Recent Developments.* Invited address to Division J of the American Educational Research Association, Chicago.

Ralushai, N.V., M.G. Masingi, D.D.M. Madiba, *et al.* 1996. *Report of the Commission of Inquiry into Witchcraft Violence and Ritual Murders in the Northern Province of South Africa.* (To: His Excellency the Honourable Member of the Executive Council for Safety and Security, Northern Province). South Africa.

Ranger, T. 1996. "Postscript. Colonial and Postcolonial Identities." In: R. Werbner and T. Ranger (eds) *Postcolonial Identities in Africa.* London: Zed Books.

Reichardt, C.S. and T.D. Cook. 1979. "Beyond Qualitative Versus Quantitative Methods." In: T.D. Cook and C.S. Reichardt (eds). *Qualitative and Quantitative Methods in Evaluation Research.* Newbury Park: Calif.

Richardson, J. 1969. *The Policy-making Process.* London: Routledge & Kegan Press.

Roberts, G. & Edwards, A. 1991. *A New Dictionary of Political Analysis.* London: Hodder & Stoughton.

Rutherford, B. 1999. "To Find an African Witch: Anthropology, Modernity, and Witch-Finding in North-West Zimbabwe." In: *Critique of Anthropology* 19 (1), pp. 89-109.

South African Pagan Rights Alliance (SAPRA). Review: witchcraft accusations and human rights abuses in Africa. South African

Pagan Rights Alliance, 7 December 2010, http://paganrightsalliance.org.

Schmidt, M. and A. Siebane. 2000. *Witches in exile: Superstition and fear have kept the residents of Tshitwi isolated for almost a decade.* Sunday Times, 21 May.

Seymour-Smith, C. 1986. *Macmillan Dictionary of Anthropology.* London: Macmillan Press.

Siebane, A. 2000. *Witchcraft threats might have caused pensioner's suicide.* Mirror, 7 April.

Silverbladt, I. 1987. *Moon, Sun and Witches: Gender Ideologies and Class in Inca and Colonial Peru.* Princeton: Princeton University Press.

Stayt, H. A. 1931. *The Bavenda.* London: Oxford University Press.

Steadman, L. 1985. "The killing of witches." In: *Oceania* 56 (2), pp. 106-23.

Tebbe, N. 2007. "witchcraft and statecraft: liberal democracy in Africa." In: *The Georgetown Law Journal 96(1),* pp 183-286.

The National Conference on Witchcraft Violence. The Commission on Gender Equality. 6-10 September 1998. Johannesburg.

Third Draft Report on Traditional Healers. NCOP Select Committee on Social Services. December 1997.

Tsedu, M. 1989. "Anger over Ritual Death: 5 000 protest in a tense homeland." *Sowetan,* 18 July.

Van Rensburg, H., A. Fourie and E. Pretorius. 1992. *Health care in South Africa: structure and dynamics.* Pretoria: Academica.

Van Warmelo, N.J. 1989. *Venda Dictionary*. Pretoria: J.L. van Schaik.

Varkevisser, C. 1973. *Socialization in a Changing Society: Sukuma Childhood in Rural and Urban Mwanza*. Tanzania: Den Haag.

Wilson, M. 1967. *Good Company: a Study of Nyakusa Age-Villages*. Boston MA: Beacon Press.

Winter, E.H. 1963. "The Enemy Within: Ambor Witchcraft and Sociological Theory" In: Middleton *Witchcraft and Sorcery in East Africa*. London: Routledge

Yin, R. 1989. *Case study research: Design and Methods*. Newbury Park, CA: Sage.